From 1995 until 2019, Roger Lytol[...]
for some of the UK's best local new[...]
the Regional Press Awards. And a [...]
Media Awards. He isn't bitter about [...]

Praise for *Panic as Man Burns Crumpets*

'The best book I've read this year, by some margin. Brilliantly written, frequently laugh-out-loud funny, but also reflective, candid, poignant and passionate about the importance of journalism. Superb'

Chris Mason, BBC political editor

'Deserves its place in the pantheon of great books about newspapers, and the newspaper industry. A funny/sad/extraordinary tale, extremely well-told'

Sam Wallace, *Daily Telegraph*

'Refreshingly honest, engagingly self-deprecating, tremendously funny and more than a little heartbreaking. By far my favourite read of the year so far'

Mike Ward, *Daily Express* and *Daily Star*

'Lytollis writes with clarity, comically self-effacing honesty and surprising poignancy . . . It is simply the story of what it is like to love what you do, and be great at it, and to watch it collapse around you in slow motion'

Robyn Vinter, *Guardian*

'Local journalism has never seemed more exotic than in this part-memoir, part-ode to that disappearing art, which is as funny as it is endearing . . . Told with a tender fondness, the bonkers, baffling but vital world of local press is paraded with the style that it deserves'

Jonathan Whitelaw, *Sun*

'Many books written by journalists have come across my desk over the course of my time as publisher of Hold the Front Page, but I would say without any hesitation that this one is the best. Not only is it the funniest, and the best-written, it is also the most honest in terms of what it reveals about its author, and more importantly about our craft'

Paul Linford, *Hold the Front Page*

ROGER LYTOLLIS

PANIC AS MAN BURNS CRUMPETS

The Vanishing World of the Local Journalist

ROBINSON

ROBINSON

First published in Great Britain in 2021 by Robinson
This paperback edition published in 2024 by Robinson

A CIP catalogue record for this book is available from the British Library

ISBN: 978-1-47214-580-2

Typeset in Garamond by Initial Typesetting Services, Edinburgh
Printed and bound in Great Britain by Clays Ltd, Elcograf S.p.A.

Papers used by Robinson are from well-managed forests
and other responsible sources

Robinson
An imprint of
Little, Brown Book Group
Carmelite House
50 Victoria Embankment
London EC4Y 0DZ

An Hachette UK Company
www.hachette.co.uk

www.littlebrown.co.uk

In memory of Tony Greenbank.
1933–2020

Contents

Glossary of Journalism Terms   ix

Introduction   xi

1   A Suit of Armour   1

2   The Newsroom   11

3   Football Crazy   25

4   Columns and Kilroy   33

5   The Art and Craft and Chaos of Feature Writing   39

6   'Tell Me Stuff, Please'   49

7   Colour Schemes   63

8   Crossing the Border   71

9   Jordan, Boris, Strippers and Booze   81

10   Theatre Wins the Lottery . . . Literally!   91

11   Stupid Bloody Questions   95

12   Hard News   105

13   Website Woes   117

14   Chasing Glory   131

15   The Man with the Pigeon Tattoo   139

16	Takeover	147
17	Star Wars	161
18	The Incredible Shrinking Staff List	175
19	Ordinary/Extraordinary	185
20	Donald Trumped by My Friend Francis	191
21	Fancy Dress for Dogs	195
22	Nude Reporter Shares His Tip	207
23	Writers on the Storm	217
24	'What's Your Name?'	229
25	Goodbye	233
	Epilogue	243
	Afterword	250
	Acknowledgements	252
	Index	255

Glossary

Bill   1) A poster outside a shop which advertises a newspaper's best story. These have been known to backfire
when the newspaper's best story is revealed as being
shite.

2) The first name of a former *Cumberland News* deputy
editor.

Byline   'By Ant and Dec', or whoever.

Clickbait An online story that uses a misleading or deliber-
ately vague headline, often with unnecessary capital
letters and exclamation marks, to attract AS MANY
READERS AS POSSIBLE!!!

Copy   Words. Journalists refer to words as 'copy' for historical
reasons: they've always enjoyed using jargon to baffle
outsiders.

Editorial The journalism part of a newspaper business. Other
departments include advertising, accounts and binge
drinking.

Fake news 1) A false story spread mainly via the internet for political purposes or as a joke.

2) The label given by Donald Trump to any fact he
doesn't like.

Intro   The first paragraph of a story. It's called an intro because journalists are too busy to say 'introduction'. Those extra two syllables could see a deadline missed.

Snapper A photographer. The name is believed to derive from their angry reaction when someone asks if they can take a picture.

Splash The main front- or back-page story. Sometimes 'ripple' would be more appropriate.

Spread A story that runs across two pages. Often referred to, even by journalists, as a 'double-page spread'. Please tell me – how many pages could a story that runs across two pages possibly have?

Vox pop A series of brief interviews about a topical issue with members of the public in the street/a journey into the bowels of hell.

Introduction

In 2003 the *Cumberland News* editorial department's Christmas party was held at a Chinese restaurant in Carlisle. After the meal there were games, most of which culminated in men doing press-ups on the floor while women lay underneath them. On the plus side, Bernard Manning didn't perform a set and none of the waitresses was dressed as a bunny girl.

The evening was shared with staff from several local companies. When the compère said the names of factories, shops and solicitors, the rest of the room cheered. When he said, 'The *Cumberland News*,' they booed. For a more sympathetic crowd, we should have booked our party with bankers and traffic wardens.

It was pantomime malice, the kind that journalists are well used to. But if the *Cumberland News* decided to share this year's do, the booing might be more heartfelt. The early noughties, when journalists were regarded merely as sleazy and untrustworthy, are now looked back on as a golden age. The world seems more cynical now. Reporters on local papers far from any seat of power find themselves accused of political bias and lies.

Phone hacking by a few national journalists has contributed to local hacks being viewed with increased suspicion. Maybe people hear the word 'hack' and get the wrong idea. No journalist I know ever hacked a phone. Most barely have the technological knowhow to use a light switch.

Some feel a perverse pride in not understanding new computer systems. Who can take the longest to learn how to send a story to the newsdesk? Who can say 'I haven't got a clue what's happened here' the most times, while a member of the IT department stands next to them weeping?

And yet these people do valuable work, unheralded. The public rages against the decline of the NHS. Cynicism about journalists means that the collapse of newspapers – another great British institution – has barely registered. This is the media that reveals when politicians are corrupt, when a health trust has covered up negligence, when a company is responsible for the death of an employee.

But lack of trust in journalists helped to fuel fake news. We're accused of telling lies by people whose idea of a reliable source is a Facebook page run by someone living in a cave with a shotgun and a decade's supply of corned beef.

Some of journalism's wounds are self-inflicted, such as the industry's determination to give away its work online. Loss of newspaper revenue and failure to capitalise on the internet have seen income plummet, along with the quality of publications. Examples of falling standards include a *Cumberland News* story about a dog owner who was fined because their dog wasn't wearing 'a mussel'. No wonder journalists are derided more now. Although I think whoever wrote that deserves a civic reception.

This book describes life at some of the best local newspapers in Britain during their boom years, and their deterioration. Since the noughties, local papers' sales have dropped by well over half. Hundreds of papers have closed. Thousands of journalists have lost their jobs. After almost twenty-five years, I became one of them.

I didn't expect my departure to provoke widespread grief. (Actually, that statement *is* fake news.) The loss of all those journalists has been largely unmourned. We're more likely to be referred to as wankers by readers of our papers' Facebook pages than thanked for our contribution to society.

Here is an attempt to explain what went wrong and why it matters. It's also the story of what happens when someone with a social phobia takes a job that demands all too frequent contact with the public.

There's plenty about the ordinary people with amazing stories who make journalism so rewarding. Those who make it an infuriating ball ache also get a mention. All human life is here. And a dog being sick on my trousers. If only it had worn a mussel.

1

A Suit of Armour

IN my final year at university I began to doubt whether my Combined Studies degree – an unhappy marriage of English literature, sociology and politics – would have employers fighting for the right to throw money at me. Not that I had any idea what I wanted to do next. Well, I did. But continuing to sleep until noon before surfacing to watch *Home and Away* seemed a questionable career plan.

Back home in Carlisle one Saturday, three months from the end of my course, I attended a Carlisle United football match and bought a fanzine. Inside was a request for readers to send in articles. I'd never considered writing for pleasure before. At school and college it felt more like a punishment.

Next day I began to write, and surfaced several hours later with three stories: a level of productivity I had never managed before, or since. Suddenly a career had presented itself. I'd be a journalist.

After graduating with a mediocre degree in the summer of 1993, I spent months sending columns and ideas to newspapers and magazines. There was encouraging feedback, but no takers.

The following year I was accepted on to a journalism course in London. At the beginning of 1995 I moved to the capital, sharing a flat with a fellow Cumbrian. The big advantage of this arrangement was that I lived rent free. The downside: my bedroom was a cupboard under the stairs. I was Harry Potter without the

Quidditch. The room had space for a single bed and a wafer-thin mint.

I turned up for the course just a couple of times a week. It wasn't the industry-standard National Council for the Training of Journalists (NCTJ). This alternative qualification didn't seem worth very much. The thought that it might have been interesting and enjoyable anyway didn't float within a million miles of my empty young head.

For a few months, life was a rollercoaster of going to the pub and watching TV. An unusually flat rollercoaster. Then my friend's landlord turned up unexpectedly and wondered why his cupboard had a bed in it, and why the bed had a student in it. I couldn't afford to pay rent in London so I reluctantly left, intending to return soon. Two years after deciding to be a journalist, my career path was still obscured by weeds and dog dirt. I was twenty-four, unemployed, and back in my home town. (Which is actually a city – Carlisle people are touchy about that.)

Things changed when I read a column in *Today*: the tabloid which revolutionised the British newspaper industry by being printed in colour. Its weekly men's section had a column called 'Man Talk'. This was normally written by celebrities. One week there was an invitation for male readers to send in columns, 'to let us know what you think about women today'.

My offering was fuelled by my numerous romantic disappointments. I wrote that being a nice guy seemed to do me no favours and since I'd become 'a born-again bastard, my love life has never been better'. There was some truth in this. Although all that was needed for my love life to have reached new heights was to be in the same room as a woman I wasn't related to.

I wrote the column on a typewriter and posted it. This was the summer of 1995, in case that description makes younger readers think it was a century earlier. In these situations, it's traditional to say, 'And then I forgot all about it.' I did not forget all about it. I thought about little else. Had they received the column? Did they like it? Would they use it?

A week later, a journalist from *Today* rang. They did like the column and wanted to publish it. My heart soared. This felt too good to be true, like vindication after two years of getting nowhere.

My parents were thrilled . . . until the column was published. My mother said my grandmother was uncomfortable with the word 'bastard', and the part where I mentioned that the 'girl of my dreams' had slept with one of my 'lager lout, womanising friends'. It had occurred to me that my family might not want to read such things. No surprise that Nana was appalled to learn I couldn't get a shag. But how could I be a columnist without being prepared to discuss my life?

At that point, my definition of journalism was being a column-ist. I knew there was another kind of journalism, which involved interviewing people. But there was no doubt in my mind that I could make a living by writing about just two things: me, and what I thought about stuff.

I sent the *Today* column to the editor of north Cumbria's two paid-for newspapers: the weekly *Cumberland News*, a broadsheet published on Fridays, and the daily *News & Star*, a tabloid published from Monday to Saturday. They were produced by Carlisle-based CN Group and regularly won awards. The *Cumberland News*, in particular, was far above the level of most local papers. Its quality helped to attract and keep journalists who were good enough to work on bigger publications. I'd grown up reading both titles. Most local people had.

Their vast patch covered the far north-west corner of England and beyond: from just north of the Scottish border, down as far as the Lake District, across the Northumberland border in the east and to the Cumbrian coast in the west. Its towns include Workington and Whitehaven on the coast, Keswick in the Lake District, Penrith and Cockermouth just outside the Lakes, and Gretna in Scotland.

The biggest place by far is Carlisle with a population of 75,000, and half that many in its surrounding towns and villages. Many new products – including Sunny Delight, no less – have been market-tested in Carlisle because its demographic is similar to the UK's as a whole.

You have to travel 60 miles to Newcastle to find anywhere bigger. Carlisle's status as a regional centre gives it things that somewhere its size wouldn't normally have, such as a crown court, a TV station (ITV Border) and a daily paper. Its isolation, and perhaps its history of being invaded by Scots, gives Carlisle people a tendency to be suspicious. Which isn't great when you're trying to do a vox pop there.

CN Group's features editor invited me for a chat. He said that the editor liked my *Today* column and he asked if I had ideas for any more. Having spent the past two years writing columns no one seemed to want, I had plenty. It was agreed that I'd come in on the next two Thursdays and Fridays.

July 1995, a month before my twenty-fifth birthday, and I'd made it! If your definition of making it is a four-day trial at a local paper for thirty quid a day. I was delighted. This *was* my definition of making it.

Persistence had paid off: I'd contacted CN Group before but without success. Later I learned about a former staff member who had also failed in his first attempt to work there. He'd responded to this setback by getting drunk one night and urinating through the letterbox.

When the *Today* column was published, my mother had mentioned the perils of writing anything that might embarrass the family. I spent my first morning as a professional journalist writing a column that was given the headline 'Sorry Dad, I just don't have what it takes to be a sex god like you'. It concerned my dad's claims to have been a ladies' man in his youth, and how this was hard for me to live up to.

The editor was a Londoner called Keith Sutton who had worked on numerous national papers before moving north. Keith was impressively enthusiastic, veering between lavish praise for his journalists' work and a desire to know who was responsible for this steaming pile of shit. I was relieved that he liked the column about my father. It was advertised on the *News & Star*'s front page with the words 'My dad the Carlisle Casanova'.

News & Star columnists usually wrote about more serious matters. Next to their columns would be an invitation for readers to offer their views. I was mortified when this was applied to the column about my dad: 'Is this the sort of image for a father to be proud of? Phone our Talkback line or write to The Editor.' As far as I'm aware, no one responded. What could they have said? 'I would like to offer my congratulations to Mr Lytollis on having been such a stud, and my sympathy for siring such a pitiful son.'

I was living with my parents and had been worried about my mother's reaction to the column. Not worried enough to not write it, but still. Publication day came and went. She made no comment. A few days later she handed me a roll of glossy paper and said, 'Your dad's workmates had this done.'

It was a photocopy of the column, the size of a small tablecloth. I didn't know you could get photocopies that big. Dad laughed when he saw it in my room. I never thought the column would upset him. After all, he was being described in his local paper as having 'that certain something which makes the opposite sex fall at his feet in passionate abandon'. If I'd thought he would mind, I like to think I wouldn't have written it. Which is a roundabout way of saying I definitely would have.

My mother never asked me not to write about the family. She did make gentle suggestions, and left it to me to realise that I should be careful not to upset anyone. Good luck with that.

All I'd ever written was columns. On my second day, the features editor disturbed this tranquil existence. 'A survey's been published claiming that lorry drivers are ditching fry-ups for healthy options like muesli,' he said. 'Go to the local truck stop with a photographer and ask drivers about it.'

An obvious truth that I'd been denying suddenly hit me. If I was to be a journalist, I would have to speak to people. This was bad news. I'd spent my three years at university largely in my room. Before going to the kitchen or bathroom I'd stand with my ear to the door, emerging only when it sounded as if nobody was around. When getting on a bus my face would burn at the thought that anyone might be looking at me.

I'd been best man at my brother's wedding, agreeing to do it only on condition that I didn't make a speech. In his speech he referred, sympathetically, to my dread of public speaking. My face burned again with self-loathing.

Thinking you're worthless while assuming that everyone is concerned with you is a strange cocktail of low self-esteem and arrogance. Whatever the psychology behind it, my life was built on avoiding people. And my dream job demanded that I seek them out.

A photographer drove us to the truck stop by the M6 on Carlisle's northern edge. My stomach churned as if I'd just eaten a fry-up and muesli sandwich. I'd had an idea, which I shared with the snapper en route. It was possibly the best breakfast-related idea in the history of CN Group. 'None of these lorry drivers are going to like muesli, are they?' I said to him. 'So why don't we stop and buy some, then you can photograph them holding it and pulling faces as if they're going to be sick?'

He replied with a scowl. At this point I lacked the confidence to assert myself. I should have insisted that we bought muesli, even though I'd have needed to jump out of a moving car to do so.

We arrived at the truck stop. I wondered if I'd be able to get away with writing a column instead of a feature. A few light-hearted observations about the waistlines of the drivers I saw and some quips about Yorkie bars? Maybe not.

We walked in. The photographer told the manager who we were and what we wanted to do. She raised no objection to me interrogating her customers. I looked around. It reminded me of being in a nightclub: wanting to speak to people but not having the nerve. I had never chatted anyone up. And none of these gentlemen looked like my type at all.

I couldn't remember the last time I'd engaged a stranger in conversation. But I either did it right now or returned to the newsroom empty-handed, told the features editor that I'd been too shy to approach anyone, and saw my journalism career end after a day and a half.

I wandered across to a lone driver and murmured an elongated 'Er . . .' He looked up. My spiel was along the lines of 'Excuse me, I'm a journalist at the local paper. I'm writing about a survey which says lots of lorry drivers these days are eating muesli instead of fry-ups. I'm asking drivers about it. So, how about you – have you swapped fry-ups for muesli?'

'You what?'

His reaction was only partly due to my machine-gun delivery. It was an early lesson that the public aren't waiting for a journalist to turn up and ask about an issue that may have as much relevance to them as the breeding cycle of monkfish. But he talked to me. I wrote down as much of what he said as I could, having no shorthand at this stage. Then I talked to another couple of drivers. They were fine. It was fine. What had I been worried about? The public were lovely!

As we walked back to our car, I saw a driver getting into his truck. Buoyed by my newfound gregariousness, I jogged towards him and called, 'Excuse me!'

'Fuck off,' he said. 'I don't give lifts.'

It turned out that being a journalist was like wearing a suit of armour. It wasn't timid little me talking to these people. It was me with the authority of representing a newspaper, and the confidence that came from being paid to do that. Mainly it was the feeling that I was in the right job. Not that I'd never be scared again when approaching people. There would be crippling nerves many times and a sense of relief after every job. I'd pretty much be singing 'Zip-a-dee-doo-dah!' on the drive back. But now I knew I could do it.

Another lesson learned that day was how press photographers are not overburdened by a lust for life. Some jobs are greeted with a grimace, and that's if you've caught them on a good day. Otherwise they'll spit swear words and ask whose stupid idea this was. Sometimes it would be my stupid idea. I used to hope they wouldn't realise this. Eventually I snapped to one of them, 'It was *my* idea.' That'll show him, I thought – shame him into being less critical.

'It's a shit idea,' he said.

I also learned about sub-editors: the people who designed pages and wrote headlines and picture captions. They're known as subs. Or something a lot worse. One of the truckers I interviewed was from Winsford. I considered writing 'Winsford, Cheshire'. Then I decided there was no point because surely everyone already knew where Winsford is. Reading my story in the *News & Star*, I saw the words 'Winsford, Somerset'. This was the first of many occasions when subs inserted errors into my work. Of which more later, when I've calmed down about Winsford.

I was right about the lorry drivers: they didn't eat muesli. The main picture was a horribly predictable shot of a trucker eating a fry-up. We should have bought muesli.

2

The Newsroom

My four-day trial was deemed a success. I was invited to keep coming in on Thursdays and Fridays, on a freelance basis, to write columns and light news stories, such as people taking part in charity events. My lack of training spared me from hard news duties like court reporting, which was a relief. I was always more interested in poking around behind the scenes than in the crash, bang, wallop of a news story. I soon began to write features: longer stories that usually involve profiling somebody or examining an issue.

Most newspaper journalists have completed an NCTJ course covering things such as media law and shorthand. I fell through the cracks, walking in with a pretty meaningless qualification and learning as I went along. My enthusiasm battled with my shyness. Speaking to people was challenging, but I loved writing. My brain felt more closely connected to my fingers than to my mouth.

Being part of the daily miracle of filling a newspaper, and the camaraderie this created, was hugely enjoyable. I'd left school at sixteen after failing my O levels. Before returning to education I'd washed cars, worked in a factory making tins for chocolates and talcum powder (those were separate tins, thankfully) and sorted post at Royal Mail. I'd lasted two days delivering post because I couldn't work out how to use elastic bands to hold bundles of letters together. My lack of practical skills is one reason why none of those jobs was enjoyable. Another reason was the feeling that I didn't fit in.

The newsroom was different. Its climate of dark humour felt like home. Much of the day passed to a soundtrack of laughter and the journalists' mantra: 'For *fuck's* sake!'

This was often heard around 11 a.m., when the first copies of that day's paper had been bought and readers began phoning with complaints. Heaven help us if the wrong crossword clues or TV listings had been printed. When the first such call came in, whoever answered it would break the news to the rest of us. There'd be a collective groan. Throughout the day I'd hear colleagues on the phone apologising.

Most complaints were from people who featured in court reports, or members of their families. One news editor looked forward to these calls. He'd lean back in his chair, put his feet on his desk and boom across the newsroom, 'Well, if you're not happy about being in the paper, maybe you shouldn't have stolen those razors!' He used that particular phrase only with people who'd stolen razors, in case you're wondering. It would have been great if he'd said it to everybody.

One day someone rang to say that a stain on their wall looked like a celebrity. I was told that we received calls like this every few years. I can't remember who any of the stains were supposed to look like. But the resemblance always turned out to be question-able, to say the least.

Despite having suffered let-downs with similar stories, our news editors were very excited by the call. This most cynical of species became like children on Christmas Eve. The stain on the wall was immediately earmarked for the following day's page three: a page reserved for quirky stories. A reporter and photographer were dispatched, returning to an eager 'Well?' from the news editors.

'It looks nothing like them.'

'Shit.'

The pictures confirmed it. This was not the face of Jesus, Elvis or Mother Teresa. This was a stain on a wall. There wasn't time to conjure up an alternative story. So next day's page-three exclusive revealed that somewhere in Cumbria lived someone with strong wishful thinking and weak eyesight. For these stories we'd always invite even more ridicule than was strictly necessary with a head-line such as 'Is *this* the face of Elvis?' Eager phone calls informed us that it wasn't.

Local papers were a weird world. Peter Hill, an ex-feature writer who now worked on sport, had once been sent to southern Spain to interview expats for a series of stories called 'Costa del Cumbria'. One subject was a former Carlisle nightclub owner, who explained that he was an astral traveller who had regular out-of-body experiences. He claimed his image had been seen back in Carlisle. He lived in a village called Mijas, and was known there as 'The Mijas Messiah'. That phrase appeared in Peter's feature and was used as its headline.

After it was published, this man wrote to the editor asking for a clarification to be printed. It appeared with the headline 'Former nightclub boss not the messiah'. The text said he 'would like to point out that he is not the messiah and only Jesus Christ can be referred to as such. We apologise for any misunderstanding.'

The number of letters and calls of all kinds added to the impression that everyone read what we wrote. In 1995 the *News & Star* sold about 28,000 copies a day and the *Cumberland News* 37,000 a week. Each paper was read by an average of three people, giving them a huge reach. The *News & Star*'s slogan used to be 'At the heart of your community'. Back then, it was true.

***

Some reporters, especially those who wrote about crime, fitted the stereotype of the hard-bitten hack who thrives on confrontation and relishes sticking their foot in the door of a reluctant interviewee. Years of writing about dark subjects and being lied to and hated could diminish anyone's sunny side. I'd hear reporters be charming on the phone, finishing with 'Thanks for your time, great to speak to you, bye!' The second they hung up, they'd mutter 'Wanker', much to my amusement.

Cutting humour was aimed at colleagues and some of those we wrote about. Even compliments carried a hint of insult. Talkative interviewees who could always be counted on to fill plenty of space would be referred to as 'a gob on a stick'.

To my relief, I wasn't the only reserved one in the newsroom. Several reporters were quiet. There were clearly other ways to interview people than yelling through their letterbox. Some reporters weren't as ruthless as they'd have their bosses believe. For many, the worst part of the job was the death knock: going to the home of a recently bereaved family in search of a quote and a picture of the deceased. Thankfully I never had to do that. It wasn't unheard of for a reporter to drive there, sit outside for a few minutes, then come back and say that the family didn't want to speak.

With one or two others, I wouldn't have been entirely surprised if they'd stood outside the local hospice with a pen and pad, asking everyone who emerged if they'd just lost a loved one.

The newsroom housed a diverse cast of characters. Some had worked on national papers before coming to Cumbria for a quieter life. They'd travelled the world and were now sitting with people whose career had never taken them beyond Penrith. And me, for whom Penrith remained a distant dream.

What most of us had in common was a tendency for messiness. Desks were strewn with newspapers, notebooks and press releases.

This could have serious consequences. One reporter found a letter under a mountain of paper. It had been sent to him from prison by a criminal he'd written about. He read aloud from it. '"Please help me overturn this unjust conviction . . . you are my last hope . . . " I'd forgotten about this. When did he write it . . . six years ago? Bollocks. I think he's dead now.'

I was a hot-desker, in the happy days before that phrase existed. Every Thursday and Friday I'd be shown to a different mass of paper teetering around a different computer screen. It was hard to find an unoccupied desk, such was the number of staff employed in the 1990s.

The newsroom was a large, open-plan space occupying most of the upstairs of the grimly functional early-1970s building. About seventy people packed into it. Reporters, feature writers and photographers were often out on jobs. The twenty or so sub-editors were destined to leave only for the toilet, the smoking room – a forbidding place of orange plastic chairs and brown-stained walls – or the canteen.

Many staff, myself included, stayed in the canteen for longer than the designated half-hour lunch break. A pool table was among the attractions. Nearly every afternoon I'd manage at least one game. I worked hard most of the time but there was still a feeling that I was getting away with something. Not so much in the games of pool: more in being paid for doing what I enjoyed in the company of the intelligent, the eccentric and the amusingly irritable.

One reporter taped a plastic bag filled with manure to the underside of a colleague's desk. Disappointed by the lack of aroma, she cut a hole in the bag and kept increasing its size until her target spent his days opening windows and spluttering, 'What's that fucking smell?'

A veteran reporter kept a leather flying helmet on his desk. Now and again I'd look up to see him typing away while wearing it, with no explanation.

Several colleagues remembered those not-so-distant days of lavish expenses and liquid lunches. I heard about former employees who would nip out for lunch and not be seen again that day.

The old-school journalists included a news editor who'd been around the block a few hundred times. When I asked him how much he wanted me to write, his usual reply was 'Enough to paper the shithouse wall.' Despite my pleading, he never revealed the size of this shithouse.

We wrote a lot of stories about wind farms. This news editor didn't think that form of energy was particularly viable, declaring, 'The average wind turbine produces enough power to wank off a gnat.'

A local celebrity rang me to report that one of his fans had named her gerbil after him. Did I want to write a story about this? I did not. But I didn't have the nerve to tell him. 'I'd love to write about it,' I said, 'but I'll just have to check with my boss.'

I explained the situation to the news editor and asked, 'What should I tell him?'

'Tell him to fuck off.'

He could be kind as well, mentoring young journalists such as myself with advice about what we'd written.

'Your intro on that story about the recycling centre . . .'

'Yes?'

'It's as flat as a witch's tit.'

I watched and listened, picking up the jargon, learning how the papers and their creators ticked, wary at first before daring to chip in to conversations. I loved being on the receiving end of piss-taking. This felt like a sign that I'd been accepted and was liked.

Or maybe hated.

During a handful of interviews, when I flipped over the page I was writing on to reach a blank one, something surprising greeted me. The next page wasn't blank. Scrawled across it were a cock and balls, rendered in impressive detail. Whoever had done this – there were several suspects – was pitching me into a game of Russian roulette. They had no way of knowing who I'd be interviewing when I turned that page.

Usually it was a phone interview, so I could hide my stunned reaction. Once, I was in the office of a therapist who practised neuro-linguistic programming. I thought about asking her what kind of person would draw a cock and balls on a colleague's notebook, and whether neuro-linguistic programming might be able to help that person. Mainly, though, I struggled to think of any questions at all as I spent the rest of the interview with that cartoon cock tattooed on my brain.

Being on, or just behind, the front line of news was thrilling. Although I didn't want to write news, I still felt the buzz when word came through of a big story, such as a body being found, and the police were telling us things the public didn't know yet. Everyone in a newsroom knows that hard news is the lifeblood. Features and columns are the knees and the genitals. You can live without them, but you'd miss them if they weren't there.

I was at the mercy of the features editor – a placid chap – and the numerous news editors. The old-school news editor won any tug of war for my services. He regarded features as the athlete's foot and the dandruff of the newsroom. When he needed some-one to drop what they were doing and run any kind of journalistic errand, he'd turn to me.

One December he wanted somebody to be photographed in a

Santa suit at a GP surgery to illustrate a story about the winter flu jab. He had the suit. All he needed was someone to wear it. He looked around the newsroom and threw it at me.

'Go to the surgery with a snapper and put this on.'

'But I've got loads to do! There's no way I can—'

'Put the suit on.'

One child cried when they saw me in the waiting room. My tentative 'Ho! Ho! Ho!' didn't help.

Occasionally I was employed as a getaway driver. We needed photographs of defendants leaving Carlisle Crown Court. If they were thought to be potentially violent, a photographer would take pictures from the back of a car across the street: a car driven by me. When they said, 'Go!' I'd zoom off. This seemed a bit melodramatic. But having grown up with cops and robbers shows like *The Sweeney*, it was a dream come true.

The old-school news editor never seemed convinced that I was busy. After reporting from a Buddhist centre, I made the mistake of telling him that one of the monks had said I had 'a great stillness'.

'He's not fucking wrong,' he replied.

The news editors and their deputies each worked for either the *Cumberland News* or the *News & Star*. All other staff worked for both papers. News editors' duties included finding stories, assigning stories and deciding when and where to use them.

The art of persuasion was useful for a news editor. One of them used to approach with an unconvincing smile. 'I think you'll like this one!' they'd say, before describing a job which would be less enjoyable to write than your mother's obituary.

I preferred brutal honesty. Other news editors would say, 'Look, this job's a bit crap – sorry. I'll try to give you something decent next time.'

In those days there were no websites to constantly feed. When an edition was finished the pressure eased for a while. People would spin their chairs towards each other and talk. Conversation topics included one that continues to intrigue me: what do people want in newspapers?

'We need more faces,' somebody would say, meaning we need more pictures of people. Everyone would nod. It soon became clear that saying 'We need more faces' was an easy way to convey an aura of expertise. Once when a news editor asked for thoughts on that morning's *News & Star*, I ventured, 'It could do with a few more faces.' I hadn't even seen the paper. But everyone nodded. I felt like a god.

News editors, like sub-editors, were usually former reporters. Most were middle aged. Reporters and feature writers ranged in age from twenties to sixties. This matched our readership's broad demographic, in the days when people under fifty still read newspapers.

Some reporters wanted to be feature writers. Others saw us as an airy-fairy adjunct to the real business of a newspaper. The old-school news editor referred to the features department as 'Sleepy Hollow'.

Reporters boasted about how quickly they'd written a splash. This had shades of 'My dad's bigger than your dad.' I heard someone claim that they'd written a *News & Star* splash in two minutes. I've spent more than two minutes searching for the right word to describe someone's eyes, before settling on 'blue'.

I'd tell reporters that feature writing is a marathon, not a sprint. We need to tuck in behind the Kenyan pacemaker before making a break from the Ethiopians with half a mile to go. Not the best analogy I ever came up with, admittedly.

***

Seeing my name in the papers I'd read for most of my life was a strange experience. The first piece to be published was the column about my dad. I remember walking through the centre of Carlisle that day, seeing the *News & Star* in shops, watching people read it and expecting the world to change. My world did. My picture sat alongside my columns and some of my other stories. People began to recognise me and were often complimentary.

Journalism, even on a local paper, seemed to be seen as a relatively glamorous job. After years of struggling to approach women on nights out, they struck up conversations about things I'd written. That boosted my confidence. I became well-known in my home town (sorry – city), which helped to give me a sense of identity.

It wasn't all cosy chats about how I came up with ideas. Journalists joke that this would be a great job if it wasn't for the public. Well, half-joke. As well as angry phone calls to the newsroom there were also calls from those who were regarded as nutters, pains in the arse, or both.

One man regularly rang to claim that decades earlier he'd been wrongly convicted and spent several years in prison as a result. We had written about this but some of my colleagues saw him as a nuisance. Once when he rang, the call was put through to me. I hadn't spoken to him before so apparently it was my turn to suffer.

I listened for about ten minutes without getting a word in. This was ridiculous: I had things to do. Annoyed by his whingeing and at being stitched up, I put the phone down. Perhaps this was my attempt at being a hard-nosed reporter who didn't take any crap. It didn't go well. He instantly rang another reporter, who marched across to my desk and angrily asked if I'd just hung up on the man. I blushed. 'No – we got cut off.' I said the same to him when she transferred the call to me. He didn't believe me and was furious.

Maybe I should have listened to him more carefully. Years later it turned out that he'd been telling the truth. His conviction was quashed. I'd kept his phone number on a list of people I didn't want to speak to. These were mainly people who had been unhappy with something I'd written. Or, more often, I was worried that they might be unhappy. If their number flashed on my phone, I'd ignore their call. They could always leave a message.

Most colleagues took a more professional approach. Not only did they always answer their own phones, they answered other people's. I'd see them sprint across the newsroom to pick up a ringing phone on a vacant desk. I stopped doing this early, when those calls were invariably from readers complaining that their paper hadn't been delivered or wanting to know what time a chemist opened.

I didn't mind people phoning to complain about my stories . . . I'll rephrase that. I *did* mind people phoning to complain about my stories. I minded it very much. But I was more irritated by the phoning than the complaining. Why couldn't they write to me? I'd written to them, indirectly. I certainly hadn't rung them at work when they were racing to meet a deadline. Or preparing to have a game of pool in the canteen.

People turning up unannounced at reception was another interaction too far for someone like me who thrived on predictability: exactly the wrong mindset for a journalist. Having said that, few of my colleagues skipped gleefully downstairs when a call came through that someone wanted to speak to a reporter.

Some reporters refused to go downstairs if someone they'd written something unflattering about turned up. One of the good things about working on features was that people generally didn't want to kick your head in. But I wasn't immune from being dispatched when the receptionist rang a news editor to say that someone wanted a reporter.

There were nearly twenty reporters and only five feature writers, including my part-time contribution. A news editor would still happily send a feature writer to see an unexpected visitor, if the features editor was looking the other way. Because people turned up in reception for all sorts of reasons. And having a great story was rarely one of them.

People did wander in with thrilling tales of personal achievement and corporate cover-up. Usually, though, all you'd get was the revelation that a bring-and-buy sale was about to be held. That was fine if they gave you the details and buggered off. But some just kept talking and I was too polite to stop them.

One morning I was sent downstairs to meet an elderly man. He handed me a bundle of paper. 'I've written a poem,' he said. 'It came to me last night. I've never written a poem before.'

I read this account of him walking down a long road as he pondered what life is all about. I was wondering that myself. 'Man writes poem' didn't seem a great story, even by my standards. So I asked about his life, hoping there'd be something worth reporting. There wasn't. He talked for twenty minutes while I fretted about all the work waiting for me upstairs.

I escaped by promising I'd try to write something about the poem. I didn't, and he never came back to ask if I had. Maybe unburdening himself was enough. That was often the case with these cold callers, and I felt for those who may have had no one else to talk to. I just didn't want to spend hours listening to them. I'd walk through reception and see a stone-faced colleague being talked at by someone. My sympathy was particularly acute if this person was holding a carrier bag stuffed with documents.

Sometimes weighty brown envelopes landed on my desk. One of my stories had touched on a reader's pet subject. Now they were telling me about it in pages of closely typed or – please, have mercy – handwritten detail, accompanied by photocopies of letters they'd sent to the relevant authorities. Whatever my strengths as a journalist may have been, sifting through a forest of paper to determine whether a story lurked within was not among them. I'd dump these documents on the desks of reporter colleagues and wonder if this attitude made me a bad human being as well as a bad journalist.

Some correspondents revelled in being cryptic. I'd written about a man who'd turned his shed into a pub. A reader wrote to tell me that they kept an old British Army tank in their shed, and enclosed a picture of it. They included no name or address: just the first half of their postcode. 'Can you find us?' the letter asked. No, I couldn't.

A Christmas card posted in January had a baffling message about Radio 1 DJ Chris Moyles, London and football. A letter about striking council workers ended with the words 'Perhaps the old saying "The good is the enemy of the best" maybe relevant. Think it through – best for whom, and for what reason?' Bletchley Park's codebreakers came out of retirement for that one.

One envelope contained part of a *Daily Mail* front page with the headline 'Fight for Britain Prime Minister' and the words '*Mail* poll shows huge majority want powers back from EU'. I suspected the sender wanted me to swim to Brussels and attack Jacques Delors with a Cumberland sausage.

3

Football Crazy

As well as Thursdays and Fridays, there was also weekend work. Editor Keith Sutton wanted me to give a supporter's perspective on Carlisle United with the kind of writing I'd been doing for the fanzine.

It was an interesting time at the club, largely thanks to its owner. Michael Knighton had come to the sporting world's attention in August 1989. Announced as the new owner of Manchester United, Knighton strode on to the Old Trafford pitch before the first game of the season. Wearing shorts and a tracksuit top, he did kick-ups and blasted balls into the net. Within weeks the media was claiming that he couldn't raise the money. Knighton denied this. Either way, the deal was off. In 1992 he set his sights somewhat lower by buying Carlisle United.

Shortly before Knighton arrived as owner and chairman, Carlisle had narrowly avoided being relegated from the Football League. By the time I arrived at the *News & Star* three years later, he'd inspired a revival. Carlisle had just been promoted to Division Two: confusingly, the third of the league's four tiers.

At the start of that 1995–6 season Knighton saw a chance to capitalise on his club's success. He launched a Sunday paper called *Borders on Sunday*, promising exclusive Carlisle United content. It covered the same area as our publications. By no coincidence whatsoever, as *Borders on Sunday* launched so did the *Sunday*

News & Star. CN Group was determined to crush Knighton's paper.

My contributions to the *Sunday News & Star* included a Carlisle United column written under the byline 'John Blunt'. The name reflected the content. It was a short, no-frills match report followed by player ratings and marks out of ten. I heard that Carlisle's players became obsessed with these. I used to think it bizarre that they could get worked up about a sequence of brief assessments that I rattled off in a couple of minutes.

Good shift – 7 / Below par – 5.

Then I realised that I'd be the same if my performance was similarly judged after every day at work.

Asked painfully obvious questions – 4 / Used too many clichés – 3.

Saturday matches finished shortly before 5 p.m. The John Blunt column had a 5.30 deadline. Email wasn't widely available in 1995. I had to ring one of CN Group's copytakers, whose jobs included typing what journalists read to them over the phone. That made me feel like a proper hack. Much of their work was with journalists calling from courts to report a verdict, probably while wearing a grubby mac and a fedora with a press card tucked in the brim.

I watched matches from the terraces rather than the press box. And I didn't have a mobile phone: they too were a rarity back then. So for home games I came to an arrangement with a friend whose parents lived next to Carlisle's Brunton Park stadium. I'd sit on their stairs with the mug of tea and the KitKat that her mother brought me, and spend twenty minutes writing my match report and ratings before phoning them in.

Very hospitable – 8.

For away matches I travelled with friends in a car or on a supporters' club bus. On the way back I'd borrow one of these friends' primitive mobiles, and try not to poke anyone's eye out with its enormous antenna.

Potential legal action – 1.

I also wrote a Carlisle United column under my own name. 'View from the Terraces' was a fan's-eye perspective of every match. Carlisle is just seven miles from the Scottish border. Games at south coast clubs such as Torquay and Bournemouth involved round trips of more than seven hundred miles. For these distant journeys we'd set off at 6 a.m. and return around midnight, drained after a diet of service-station food and disappointing football.

During one match at Burnley the loudspeakers crackled into life. My heart thumped as the announcer said, 'Will Roger Lytollis contact the nearest steward? Roger Lytollis to the nearest steward, please.' I was mortified. There were almost ten thousand people in the stadium. Having attention drawn to myself in real life, rather than on the page, was my worst nightmare. I shuffled to a steward and told him that the announcement had been for me. I was too embarrassed to realise that this might be bad news. Maybe someone had died?

Another steward led me to an office and I was handed a phone. It was one of the news editors. He couldn't contact the freelance photographer who was covering the game for us: could I find him and ask him to send his pictures that night rather than tomorrow?

Back at work the following week, I told the news editor how embarrassed I'd been to hear my name announced to thousands of people. A few weeks later, standing on the away fans' terrace at Shrewsbury Town, a voice came over the loudspeakers. 'Will Roger Lytollis contact the nearest steward?' I didn't move, despite the announcement being repeated several times. In the newsroom a few days later the news editor stifled a smile as he asked if I'd enjoyed the match. 'Yeah, it was great, thanks,' I replied.

The same announcement was made at the next few away games. The only variation was the announcer's attempt to pronounce my surname. It was like one of those warning messages made to staff using code words. For people in the know, 'Will Roger Lytollis contact the nearest steward?' meant 'The news editor is laughing hysterically at the discomfort he's causing hundreds of miles away.'

Working for sport was enjoyable. The department occupied six desks on one side of the newsroom, next to a waist-high wall. Its staff had made a valiant effort to separate themselves from the rest of the room by covering this wall with piles of books and luxuriant potted plants.

Sport played by its own rules. The atmosphere was light-hearted with much emphasis on coming up with puns in headlines and intros. When Carlisle United signed an Icelandic player, our United reporter was instructed to ask him whether he had ever eaten whale meat and, if so, would he consider consuming it again. The reporter returned with the news that the player had once eaten whale meat and did not rule out repeating this experience. The sub-editors were jubilant. Next day the back-page headline was 'Whale meat again'.

My football writing was well received by many Carlisle fans. They seemed to appreciate that I was a fellow supporter who'd followed the team for years. Carlisle's players were less happy with some of my writing . . . although they didn't know it was mine. When I met any players their first comment was usually criticism of John Blunt, often using rhyming slang. They'd then ask me who he was. 'I've no idea,' I replied.

Hiding behind a pseudonym – 3.

In a football column written under my own name, I described a former player as one of Carlisle's worst ever. This prompted a letter to the editor from one of his ex-teammates. He said the player in question had been greatly upset by my comment. That hit me hard. I wrote to the player who'd written the letter, apologising profusely and asking him to tell his friend that I didn't really think he was that bad.

This did not have the desired effect. The player sent another letter to Keith Sutton – and enclosed a copy of my letter to him. I was summoned by the assistant editor, who wasn't impressed that I'd written to a reader to claim that what I'd said in my column was a load of rubbish. He warned me never to apologise unless it could be proven that I'd written something factually inaccurate. He seemed disappointed to find that this young gun who'd been hired for his strong views was actually rather sensitive. In my gung-ho approach, it hadn't occurred to me that my words had the power to hurt.

The matter ended there, unlike my feud with Michael Knighton. *Borders on Sunday* had lasted just a few weeks before being seen off by the *Sunday News & Star*. Carlisle United were struggling, and were eventually relegated. My football columns improved Knighton's mood even more. They criticised him for not investing in the squad and for selling its best players too cheaply.

Knighton's demeanour reminded me of Margaret Thatcher. Both seemed to derive great pleasure from speaking, with the certainty that they were right and that the audience would be grateful for the lesson. Having been vilified by many sports journalists over his aborted attempt to buy Manchester United, Knighton might have expected a quiet time at Carlisle. I must have been an almighty pain in the arse, repeatedly asking in print why he'd sold this player or why he hadn't bought that player. Or that one. Or that one.

Our first encounter came when I'd been at CN Group for six months. No outsider ever entered the newsroom unless they were accompanied by a member of staff, until the afternoon Knighton barged in. 'I'd like a word with you, young man,' he said. I can't remember the specifics. But in summary he suggested that I didn't know what I was talking about and should perhaps seek alternative employment.

For the next few weeks most people who'd been there at the time, and many who hadn't, greeted me by saying, 'I'd like a word with you, young man.' No one had said anything while he was monstering me. They were too busy gleefully gawping. Quite right too: I'd have done the same.

Knighton's visit didn't deter me. Several weeks later Carlisle's best young player, Paul Murray, was rumoured to be on the verge of being sold to a Premier League club. In one column I wondered if he'd been allowed to play while not fully fit at a match that was watched by the manager of Liverpool. I wrote that United seemed so eager for Murray to play, 'It wouldn't have been surprising to see the chairman pushing him around the pitch in a wheelchair.'

Knighton often wrote to the *News & Star* to criticise me. At first I took this personally, rather than appreciating that he had every right to reply to my comments. Then again, sometimes it was personal.

One of his letters described my writing as 'the garbled yappings of a pip-squeak'. He expressed himself even more colourfully in the club's matchday programme, writing lengthy columns criticising the local media, especially me. In one of these I was referred to as 'a sneaky little creep'. In another he wrote of me: 'Tis he who must lead the crusade to see the Chairman slain. Slain according to the righteous moral high ground of the new Titan, wielding his titanic hammerhead God-like to smash the Anti-Christ into unconditional submission.'

I struggled to get my head around that one. I asked a friend for his interpretation. 'He's saying you're a twat,' he explained.

One anonymous column in the programme mocked my unsuccessful job application a few years earlier to work in the ticket hut at a local golf course. The column had the desired effect of making me feel humiliated. My colleagues loved the fact that someone as well-known as Knighton was annoyed by someone as obscure as me. Knighton accused me of trying to use him to make a name for myself. It wasn't true, although he raised my profile with his florid responses to my writing.

I wasn't the only journalist he disliked. In 1996 he claimed that a *News & Star* splash quoted him speaking off the record: something the reporter denied. Knighton had talked of an experience years earlier when he'd seen a UFO and heard a voice say, 'Michael, don't be afraid.' The subsequent story and headline – 'Knighton: "Aliens spoke to me"' – didn't exactly thrill him. He threatened to resign from the club in protest.

The following year his latest objection to something I'd written took a novel form. Posters appeared around Brunton Park. These featured my photo under the words 'Unwanted – Man Behaving Sadly'. They referred to me as 'U.F.O. – Un-Friendly Orifice' and said I was 'Unaffectionately known at Brunton Park as "Dodgy Halitosis"'.

The posters went on to describe me as 'an unwelcome alien entity. If spotted around/over Brunton Park please beam up to nearest Steward/Club Official who are programmed to zap and eliminate by escorting politely from our space – our sacred Brunton Park. If entity has pen in hand – DO NOT APPROACH – CONSIDERED DANGEROUS.'

Not for the first time, I wasn't sure what to make of Knighton's words. Keith Sutton decided I should pose for a picture outside Brunton Park, while wearing an alien mask. This became a *News & Star* splash with the headline 'Knighton versus the alien'. The *Sunday People* ran a story about our feud: '"Unwanted" soccer fan is over the moon!'

4

Columns and Kilroy

I N my first year at CN Group I wrote columns most weeks about pretty much whatever I felt like. One of these concerned the royal family. Why do we need them, why should we pay for them, and other startlingly original observations. To my surprise, letters poured in.

Idiotic, ill-informed rubbish.

Someone who looks as if he lives on garlic and can't stand the smell of his own armpits.

He wants to keep his big mouth shut. If he does not like the Royal Family he should get the hell out of Britain.

Send him to Siberia for good.

I hope he gets what he deserves.

I know a lot of people would do him harm if they caught him.

By his photo in the News & Star he won't be much older than 40, the bloody upstart. [The photo was taken when I was twenty-four.]

This reaction shook me. How ridiculous that people could get so worked up by someone saying they're not a fan of the royal family. How disturbing that their love of the royals comes with such bile. The confidence that journalism had given me increased my self-esteem only so far. Criticism opened up old insecurities.

My colleagues' joyful reaction to these letters and their subsequent piss-taking helped me see the funny side. Another comfort was learning how much editors love that kind of feedback, hence the presence of so many gob-on-a-stick columnists in the national press.

In one self-deprecating column about dating, I mentioned the difficulty I'd encountered in unhooking bras. One reader penned the following response:

> I have just read Lytollis's article on women's bras and I feel physically sick. On page 28 there are photos of Bonny Babies [a longstanding *News & Star* feature with cute kids]. There's Stacey, Jemima, Kelsey and Jessica, lovely, lovely girls. What does the future hold for them? Are they to be stalked by predators like Lytollis, full of sexual lust, just waiting to tear off their bras? What is the world coming to? Is there no respect for womanhood?

After reading that, I realised one of us needed psychiatric help. I'm still not sure which one.

My early columns featured some painfully predictable targets. I said of Miss World, 'Banished by terrestrial TV, the annual celebration of women in their bikinis is now being shown on Sky.' A few days later a fax arrived from Eric Morley: Miss World's creator.

He wrote, 'In 1952 I banned bikinis and they have been banned ever since, so where on earth have you been all these years?'

I thanked Eric for his response and, in contrast to the mocking tone of my column, suggested that perhaps I could report from the next Miss World contest to give the inside story. He replied, 'I would not like to put you to the trouble of a ten-hour flight to the Seychelles.' No trouble at all, Eric.

I don't remember writing a column about Cliff Richard, but I must have done. The evidence is a reader's letter about him in a folder at home, which ends with the words, 'Cliff will be remembered and loved long, long after Roger Lytollis is gone.' Firm but fair.

My columns were normally light-hearted, often reflecting my lifestyle of going out and trying to meet women. Keith Sutton decided to give me a weekly column along these lines. I suggested the title 'Man Behaving Badly', in reference to the BBC sitcom *Men Behaving Badly*. Week after week I trotted out tales of my dating hell. Although I made laddish references to the fairer sex, the butt of the joke was usually me. At the end of the column I'd be the one crying alone.

The producer of BBC talk show *Kilroy* was from Carlisle. He had read my column and enjoyed it. I discovered this when he rang me at home one morning in 1997. 'We're recording a programme in London tomorrow,' he said. 'It will have the theme "Can men survive without women?" We have some well-known women taking part.' He mentioned a Page Three model and a Gladiator. I sensed that this wasn't going to be *Newsnight*.

'We're looking for two men to stir things up and explain why men can easily survive without women. Reading some of the lines in your column, I think you could be one of those men. What do you reckon?'

I heard myself say 'Maybe' instead of 'I'd rather die of syphilis.' I was flattered to be asked. And this could be a way to overcome my fear of public speaking. An extreme way, admittedly. But if it went well it could change my life.

The producer then tested me with the big question. 'So, Roger . . . can men survive without women?' The honest answer would have been, 'In my case, no. I need women to bolster my fragile ego and to fill the aching void in my soul.' Instead, I gave him what he wanted. 'We can easily survive without women, as long as we have a microwave and a dishwasher.'

The producer laughed. I agreed to appear on the show and he explained the travel arrangements. I put the phone down and thought, *Shit – what have I done?*

A memory from my university days returned. Back then I'd talked to a counsellor about the panic attacks I had whenever I was due to speak in a tutorial. Speaking in public – by which I mean more than two or three people – felt like an out-of-body experience. I'd be watching myself and thinking, *Come on then – how are you going to do this?*

The counsellor had suggested beta blockers: pills which slow the heart rate and lower blood pressure, reducing anxiety. I'd never taken them but this seemed like a good time to start. I rang my GP surgery and secured an appointment that afternoon: you can tell this was a while ago. The doctor listened as I described the hole I'd clambered into. Basically: 'I'm going to be on telly but I don't want to be on telly but it could help my career but not if my bowels explode on camera.' He prescribed me beta blockers, with a warning to take just one.

I travelled to London on a sleeper train, which left Carlisle at 2 a.m. My image of sleepers was based on black-and-white films in which overnight trains were a glamorous way to travel. I opened my cabin door. A man in a vest and Y-fronts turned and stared at me. There were bunk beds. I hadn't slept in a bunk bed since I was five. I still haven't. There would be no chance of sleep.

I spent the night on the bottom bunk, staring at my new friend's indentation in the mattress above. A feeling of dread clung to me. Even speaking on the phone at work when a handful of people could hear me was stressful. In a few hours I was expected to be wittily confident in front of TV cameras and a studio audience that included celebrities.

We pulled into Euston Station at 7 a.m. A car would be arriving at nine to take me to Teddington Studios. I wandered around for an hour then rang the producer. 'I'm really sorry,' I said. 'But I can't do it.' I explained my terror of public speaking and whimpered an apology for messing him about. He took it reasonably well. Better to find out now than after the show had started.

He asked if I'd still come to the studio to sit in the audience, which I did. Even that was nerve-wracking. I'd seen the programme before. In my memory, host Robert Kilroy-Silk would turn to audience members and ask for their thoughts. What if he did that to me? I took five beta blockers, sat on the back row, and prayed for this to be over.

My memory of the recording is mercifully vague. I do recall that the man who was going to 'stir things up' and had been left by me to fend for himself didn't fare too well in the battle of the sexes. The programme was now a bit unbalanced. I knew the feeling.

Afterwards I skulked away and met up with the friend whose cupboard I'd slept in two years earlier. We went for a few drinks, which turned into a lot of drinks. The GP had said something about beta blockers and alcohol. Take a borderline overdose then get pissed? Yeah, that was it.

By late afternoon the world had turned fuzzy. I'd had no sleep for almost thirty-six hours, not to mention my drink and drugs hell. It felt as if my pulse rate had dropped to single figures. I left the pub, climbed on to a nearby wall, and fell asleep. I slumped forward and woke just in time to land on my feet. I climbed back on to the wall, fell asleep, fell off, and woke just in time again. I repeated this cycle several times before it occurred to me that maybe I should stop climbing on to the wall.

The *Kilroy* producer isn't the only person to assume that my writing voice is the real me. Maybe it is. My speaking voice doesn't feel like mine. I prefer my writing voice. It's more confident and articulate than the other one. And writing has a delete key. Go back and make it better.

I sensed that readers were disappointed when meeting me because I wasn't the person on the page. This was expressed most forcibly on a night out by a woman who seemed to have had a few drinks. 'You're not like your column,' she said. 'You're boring.' After the shock had subsided, I felt flattered. The real me was the column. The real me wasn't boring.

5

The Art and Craft and
Chaos of Feature Writing

B Y 1998 I was in the newsroom three days a week as well as writing my Carlisle United columns. Keith Sutton decided he'd get better value if I joined the staff full-time rather than continuing to freelance. That was fine by me. After two-and-a-half years I felt like part of the team anyway.

The only training I'd had since becoming a journalist was a few media law refresher courses, to refresh what I didn't know in the first place, and shorthand. Media law is more important to reporters than to feature writers, especially those doing court reporting. Apparently, you're not supposed to say that people are guilty if they've pleaded not guilty – stuff like that. As for feature writing, someone might not like the way you described their voice, their smile or their furniture, but they'd struggle to sue you for it.

Learning shorthand was hard. This was two years of homework to master the art of drawing squiggles and deciphering them later. The squiggles were sometimes difficult to interpret. Thankfully, context revealed whether my interviewee had said pat, pet, pit, pot or put. Ideally all of them – what a sentence that would be.

I've never been taught the most important lesson: how to make people read what you've written. The best book about journalism I've read, *The Art and Craft of Feature Writing* by William E.

Blundell, includes the sobering sentence, 'Nothing is easier than to stop reading.'

With any story, the subject is more important than the style. A badly written piece about a celebrity caught dogging will be read much more keenly than a masterpiece about the chairman of a council committee. Does this mean that journalists should spend their time driving around remote lay-bys in the hope of catching an *X Factor* finalist in the act? Yes – it definitely does.

By the time I became a full-time staff member, I was writing more features than light news stories. Broadly speaking, there are three types of feature.

There's the type where an issue is analysed. Are our high streets dying? Are young people struggling to get on the housing ladder? Go out and speak to those involved. Or, more likely, stay in the newsroom and make some phone calls.

There are profiles: try to encapsulate someone's life and personality in 1,200 words or thereabouts.

And there are colour pieces: colour being the descriptive element that captures the atmosphere of the event you're writing about.

If they're not careful, a feature writer's life can be dictated by the calendar.

January: New year, new you.

February: How to woo the man/woman of your dreams on Valentine's Day.

March: Pancakes and St Patrick's Day.

April: Spring breaks and Easter eggs.

This could become depressingly predictable. January was bleak enough without the pain of finding new people to talk to about Chinese New Year and Burns Night. Some things cropped up all year round. There were times when I seemed to be writing weight-loss stories every half hour. How about weight-gain stories? 'I've put on six stone in a month – and I haven't finished yet!' I'd read it.

Coming up with my own ideas was vital. Either that or risk being landed with something that would have me, and probably the readers, in despair. Examples in my early years included a proposal to expand the Lake District National Park with a deserted strip of land that no one seemed to give a monkey's about, and something about salmon-fishing regulations on the River Eden, which I understood less than the salmon did. That's not a pleasant situation. But it can happen when the features editor doesn't have any better ideas for tomorrow's paper, and neither do you.

In the case of what the features editor dubbed 'the salmon spread', the best I could do was ring everyone I could think of who had any connection to rivers or fishing. Where's J. R. Hartley when you need him? Dress it up with an intro about the calm surface and the turmoil underneath, hope nobody reads it, and move on.

Being given jobs outside your area of expertise is an occupational hazard, especially when you don't have an area of expertise. I had a working knowledge of many topics. For many more, my knowledge was long-term unemployed.

The biggest danger came when a specialist, such as the health or education reporter, was off. I'd hear a news editor swear when they discovered that the one person who understood the issues wasn't around to interview a government minister. At this point every reporter in the room would suddenly make an urgent phone call or disappear. The stampede was most frantic when the farming reporter was away. No one else in the newsroom could tell one end of a cow from the other.

In our health reporter's absence, I was once asked to interview the chief executive of North Cumbria University Hospitals NHS Trust. The fact that I didn't know what this organisation was did not bode well. Before the interview I had an hour to read a 123-page report. It reminded me of being back at school, when my O-level history revision began in the corridor outside the exam hall. I failed that day as well.

I rushed to the interview and was greeted by the chief executive and a press officer. They knew the report, and the issues behind it, inside out. I daresay they even knew what North Cumbria University Hospitals NHS Trust was. Meanwhile I was turning up for a gunfight armed with a broken toilet brush.

It always seemed unfair when managers were accompanied by press officers. The managers were, supposedly, experts in their area. Their hand was strengthened further by press officers prompting them with facts and figures. I'd look at the press officer and think: *Your boss is paid a lot more than me to know about this subject, and you're bailing them out?* It would have been far more reasonable if they'd moved to my side of the table.

Generally, time passes much too quickly. But that was one of those jobs where I'd gladly have fast-forwarded to the end of the day, to sitting at home and wondering how I'd got through it. The chief executive seemed to be speaking Greek. The woman next to him was his interpreter. I stopped just short of saying, 'What's a hospital?' But I did ask obvious questions and received obvious replies. I lacked the knowledge to ask anything that might have led to revealing answers, or to notice any holes in the responses. All in all, a proud day for journalism.

When journalists are interviewed about their job, they usually say they love the satisfaction of holding the powerful to account or giving a voice to the underdog. I admire those who are driven by these things but I never really shared their motivation. All I wanted was to tell good stories.

Journalists are also supposed to love the job's unpredictable nature and the thrill of a breaking story. Not me. I hated being asked to lever my arse from my chair for any job that hadn't been noted in my diary at least a day before.

People have told me they suspect I'm on the autism spectrum. I'm not sure. Just because I stuck to the same routine every day: lunch at precisely noon. And just because it was the same lunch every day: tuna and sweetcorn sandwiches. That's why I never became a war reporter. It wasn't so much the danger; more the irregular meal times.

This flimsy theory was tested in 2000 when I spent a few days in Bosnia with the King's Own Royal Border Regiment, Cumbria's army regiment. The Bosnian War had ended five years earlier. I wanted the kudos without the risk. I'd be able to tell people that I went to Bosnia with the army, and hope they'd think this had involved some courage on my part. I was still nervous about going. Those journalists who arrive in war-torn countries on time impressed me more than ever.

While I loved my job, I was bothered by the knowledge that some writers pushed themselves much further. Before going to Bosnia, I read Anthony Loyd's *My War Gone By, I Miss It So*. Loyd, an ex-soldier, reported – brilliantly – from the Bosnian War and found himself drawn to its darkness.

The Things They Carried, by Tim O'Brien, based on his service in Vietnam, is the best writing I've ever read. These authors go through hell but are rewarded with inherently interesting material. The risk–reward ratio is different for us local types. A parish council meeting probably won't provide the most compelling story ever. But on the plus side (spoiler alert) it's unlikely to end in a massacre.

> Bosnia is a beautiful country. Red roofs and white walls peer through trees on densely covered green hills. Mountains are reflected in wide, twisting rivers. Cornfields sway. It's a Van Gogh landscape lifted from southern France. Except for the walls peppered by bullet holes and the roofs which are absent without leave. Bosnia is a beautiful country scarred by an ugly past.

The Border Regiment was in Bosnia to keep the peace: that was the army line. Most of the soldiers I met were stationed in a former bus depot. They seemed bored and were looking forward to their next posting, in Cyprus. For two days I interviewed soldiers, officers and local people about the war and its aftermath. On the third day I came down for breakfast and was told to pack my things.

'We're off for some R and R,' a soldier said.

'What's that?'

'Rest and relaxation.'

We'd be spending the next few days on Brač, a Croatian island in the Adriatic Sea. Some of us travelled there in a Chinook helicopter. As we flew low over a river with mountains on either side, the pilot repeatedly tilted the craft steeply left then right, left then right. Feeling ill and starting to sweat, I breathed deeply and stared at the floor. *Don't be sick*, I thought. *Don't embarrass yourself in front of all these military men.* I glanced up. Everyone was breathing deeply and staring at the floor.

We landed and ran down a ramp. A crowd of locals applauded. I felt like James Bond.

Brač was idyllic. For four days we sunbathed, windsurfed, ate and drank. I did a few interviews. But I knew the ones in Bosnia had provided more than enough for the series of features that was planned.

Back in the newsroom I told people how hard I'd worked, neglecting to mention that I'd spent most of the week on a beach. For the next few days I started work before 7 a.m. to give myself time to do the features justice. Stories of how Serbs, Croats and Muslims – formerly neighbours and friends – turned on each other during the war were devastating. I wrote three of the best features I'd ever written. A week after finishing, I asked when they'd be published. Two of them never appeared: they were lost in our computer system. That shouldn't have been possible. But our IT staff confirmed that they'd vanished.

Was it a plot by someone with a vested interest in silencing the truth about Bosnia? Not exactly. Spend enough time with newsroom technology and you learn that a story you're working on can disappear without trace. Stories that you know are in the digital archive because you looked them up yesterday cannot be found today. That alone is responsible for 23 per cent of all 'For *fuck's* sakes!' uttered in newsrooms.

The loss of two stories after so many hours of work was hugely frustrating. I couldn't face writing them again. All that remained was my piece about the soldiers. I'm sure the headline that a sub gave it – 'Bored in a bus depot in Bosnia' – will have tempted at least half-a-dozen readers to dive in.

That was one of my four trips abroad with CN Group. Two of those were to Ireland so 'abroad' is probably pushing it, even after Brexit. The other proper foreign trip came three months after Bosnia. I flew to Brussels to examine the European Parliament's impact on Cumbria and to interview the county's three MEPs. They projected an image of politicians working across national and party boundaries for the common good: a heart-warming message, which would be kicked in the bollocks by British voters sixteen years later.

An hour in the parliament's Legal Affairs Committee felt like much longer: 'A voice in the headphones revealed that the committee was discussing "the impact of community legislation on public finance". Teaspoons tinkled on saucers. I accepted a waiter's offer of coffee. There was no tea, not even for the English.'

***

A profile interview or a colour piece normally unfolded much as I expected it to. But sometimes I'd arrive and find that the person or event was somehow very different. Occasionally it paid to stick around.

Two examples: I attended a football match for a feature about a Sunday league's only female manager. In the dying moments, a man strode on to the pitch and confronted one of her players. They started punching each other. While the rest of us stood around bewildered, the manager threw herself between them to break up the fight.

I spent an afternoon on a speed awareness course, reporting what it involved and interviewing participants. As the course was about to end, the instructor revealed that he had a personal reason for encouraging safer driving. When he was nineteen, he'd been on the way to see his girlfriend when his car hit a boy aged about six who ran out in front of him.

Afterwards the instructor told me, 'On the course, I talk about what you can do in that split second. I did nothing. I hit him. His head went on top of the bonnet and he slid under the car. I'd broken his leg, his hip and his collarbone. The police didn't blame me. The parents didn't blame me. I wasn't speeding. But my mind was on my girlfriend. I could have had the speed lower. Seven years later there was a lad walking past with a limp. I remembered him . . . I crippled him.'

I wrote both those features chronologically, leaving these bits until the end. Should I have started with them, to grab readers' attention, or was it right to build to a climax? Now I'm convinced I should have started with them. People might have given up before the end. *Nothing is easier than to stop reading.*

This was all part of the feature-writing puzzle. How do I structure stories? What do I ask? How do I ask it? And how do I get the dog vomit off my trousers?

Some of the puzzles were difficult to predict and to solve. After interviewing one man, we spent a few minutes talking in his kitchen. His dog was retching. Eventually the hound vomited over the floor. Its owner didn't seem particularly concerned – unlike me, when the dog came towards me with sick hanging from the long strands of fur around its mouth. Some of this drooled on to my hand and trousers. The owner appeared oblivious. I managed to stifle swear words for the sake of what had been a good interview.

After another interview at someone's house I asked if I could use the toilet. To my horror, there was shit on the seat. The horror increased when a realisation dawned. If I didn't wipe it off, they'd assume I'd left it there. I didn't fancy them telling everyone that the man from the *Cumberland News* had shat on their toilet seat. So I cleaned it up, retching all the while.

I can't claim to have always been an innocent party in such matters, after urinating in the garden of the Worldwide President of the Mothers' Union.

Worldwide President: I'd love a job title like that. She lived in a village half an hour from Carlisle. The photographer had rung her to reschedule his visit. It turned out that she thought I'd be coming at a different time as well. I arrived at her house and no one was in. I was bursting for a pee. Her back garden was secluded with plenty of trees.

Cumbria is a large county and interviews were often a long drive away. It was usually cold, I drank a lot of tea, and council cuts had decimated our public toilets. It's remarkable that I didn't piss in more gardens.

We rearranged the interview. Not long after it was published, I received a letter from the secretary of a local Mothers' Union branch. She said that she'd enjoyed the feature and wondered if I'd like to be the guest speaker at one of their monthly meetings. She thought I'd have some interesting stories about the strange things that can happen to a journalist. I explained that my fear of public speaking meant I'd have to say no. Probably for the best.

6

'Tell Me Stuff, Please'

I'VE never been sure if I'm good at interviewing or if people would have confided the same things to anyone who happened to say, 'Tell me stuff, please.' My interview style – quiet and a bit bumbling – reflects my personality. Whenever I wished I was more dynamic, I told myself that my way of doing things relaxes people and lowers their guard. I also knew that a Jeremy Paxman interview is theatre. There's no need for a performance if no one's watching.

When writing a profile I liked to interview people at their home, unless they had the kind of job I could accompany them on, such as an Elvis tribute act. I described Stevie Las Vegas squeezing between the dressing room's sink and stacked-up chairs to peer in the mirror, slicking his hair back with tap water and gel, changing into a gold shirt and black pinstripe trousers with a belt that looked borrowed from a title-winning boxer.

He gargled water, put on his shades, and said, 'I'll get them going. I never fail.' Swinging his right arm and swaying his hips, the next words flowed out in a deep Memphis drawl. 'Let's get motivated! Rock-a-hula! Rock rock-a-hula!'

Putting the likes of Stevie in their natural environment could improve a profile by giving it an element of the colour piece. Generally, though, I thought people would be most relaxed and likely to say interesting things at home. Unfortunately, this theory may have been bollocks.

When someone comes to my home I'm far from relaxed. I'm nervous about whether the place is clean and tidy enough. I worry about what they'll think of the décor and the contents of my shelves. So maybe some people didn't spend our interview in a Zen-like state in which their subconscious roamed free. Maybe they were thinking, *If he notices that Boyzone CD I'll be mortified.*

I learned not to mention anyone's CDs in my features. This realisation came after writing profiles in which I used people's music, paintings and kitchen utensils to interpret their personality, with all the psychological insight of *Through the Keyhole*.

The big advantage of seeing someone at home is fewer distractions than in the outside world. If they had a TV or a radio on, I could politely ask them to turn it down. It was harder to do this in a café or a pub. I was put off meeting in pubs when an interview with the singer in a rock band was interrupted by an elderly man who was somewhat the worse for wear. He was convinced that I was a policeman and my interviewee was a 'grass'. My interviewee was not a grass. He was, though, tall and well-built, which helped him to defuse the situation. Even if defuse seems too gentle a word when the defusing entails telling an old man to fuck off.

Trying to impose order on profile interviews wasn't always a good idea. A woman in her eighties had run the same Carlisle preschool for fifty years and was still going strong. I visited her there, sat through registration, and waited to be shown into her office.

Instead we stayed where we were, talking to each other over the sound of toddlers laughing and crying, vying for her attention, bringing us smoothies made from play dough. For the first few minutes I was frustrated. *Oh no: she's interacting with children rather than sitting in a quiet room to talk about interacting with children.* Then it dawned on me that this was a precious glimpse into her personality.

But normally I preferred interviews to be as calm and quiet as possible. Tell me about your life, please. No interruptions. No complications. So I'd be annoyed when an interviewee showed me into a room and someone else, usually their partner, was there.

I always felt like saying, 'Yes – can I help you?' It's just as well that I didn't, considering they probably lived there. But someone else's presence made me feel inhibited. More importantly, I worried that it would inhibit the interviewee. Even if the partner said nothing, I sensed that they were there to encourage caution. My paranoia was sometimes justified. They'd interrupt an answer by saying, 'I don't think you should talk about that.' This was usually the most controversial part of the interview: often the reason I'd wanted to do it in the first place.

Resisting the urge to say, 'Mind your own business,' I'd suggest it was important that the question was answered because it helped give an insight into the issue we were discussing, or gave other people hope that it could be tackled, or whatever I could think of to ensure we weren't taken down a side road of kittens and bunny rabbits.

Interviews could also be sabotaged by my colleagues. I got on well with our photographers. Sometimes we travelled to jobs together. These journeys were an enjoyable chance to share thoughts about workmates and the wisdom, or otherwise, of managerial decisions.

The public loved snappers. They could charm people when they wanted to, a skill honed through years of asking them to do daft things on camera. Persuading students who'd received good exam results to leap in the air was a perennial favourite. And the public were fascinated by their cameras. 'What kind is it? How much was it?' All I had was a biro and a case of Pentax envy.

There were times, especially in my early days, when photographers helped me during interviews. If I was struggling to think of a question or if the interviewee just wasn't responding well, the snapper would give me a chance to regroup by making a comment about something else, or by asking a question themselves. Usually a really good question, which made me wish I'd thought of it.

But they could talk too much. I dreaded going on jobs with one photographer who saw interviews as a chance to tell his life story. The main trigger would be the interviewee mentioning any place in which the snapper had lived or worked. If they mentioned one particular city, I'd wince.

The photographer would spring to life: 'I used to live there!' He'd tell the interviewee which parts of the city he'd lived in and who he'd known. He'd ask them if they'd lived in those places and if they knew those people. The first couple of times, I was stunned into silence. Then I'd just talk over him. His interruptions were the equivalent of me jumping in front of his camera when he was trying to take a picture. He was a nice bloke, though, which made me feel even worse about wanting to bludgeon him to death.

Then there was photographers' timekeeping. If we were travelling to a job together, I'd work out when we needed to leave and ask them if we could set off then. They'd agree, and set off fifteen minutes after that time. If whoever we were seeing was irritated by our late arrival, the snapper would find a window to gaze out of while I mumbled an apology. Bastards.

At least we were on the same side, in theory. Some jobs came with competition in the shape of local TV and radio. This was BBC Cumbria, who sometimes sent TV and radio reporters to the same job, independent radio station CFM and ITV Border. These were friendly rivalries. We'd all spent enough time waiting in the rain to know that journalism generally wasn't glamorous. But there was an unofficial hierarchy. TV first, then radio, then us.

It reminded me of that 1960s sketch about the class system with John Cleese, Ronnie Barker and Ronnie Corbett. I was Ronnie Corbett, at the bottom of the pile. I looked up to them because they were on the telly and the wireless. They looked down on me because the medium I broadcast on was fish-and-chip wrapping.

In the noughties we did launch some kind of TV show. This was a daily news bulletin, which appeared on our website. A handful of reporters fronted it. I was never asked, although the sight of me trying to hide under the desk might have been entertaining. The studio was a cupboard just off the newsroom, which was one reason why this short-lived venture gained the unofficial title 'Tinpot Telly'.

When I was out on jobs with other journalists, TV reporters nearly always did their interviews first. Maybe this was for technical reasons to do with the time needed for editing, dubbing and filming themselves nodding at the interviewee. Mainly, though, it was a sign of the hold that telly had over us newspaper hacks. Or me, anyway. Telly seemed mysterious and magical.

I was amused by the contrast between broadcasters' staid on-air personas and the foul-mouthed versions of them that I knew. It was like the sanctimonious attitude of our papers to swearing compared with the obscenities that spewed from most of us in the newsroom. I smuggled the occasional arse into homes around Cumbria. But anything stronger – even a f*** – was out of the question.

Interviewing people in their home followed a broadly predictable path. They'd usually offer me tea or coffee. If they didn't offer me anything, I'd try not to let it jaundice my view of the miserable twat. Unless time was very limited, I'd warm them up with a question such as, 'How long have you lived here?' I hoped this would help to relax them. The answer also gave a useful clue to how the interview would progress. If they said something like, 'Well, we moved here in August 1992. It was a fortnight before Sarah's wedding. Sarah's my eldest. She got married the first weekend in September and . . .' I'd start to panic.

I'd think, *Bloody hell – if 'How long have you lived here?' is taking this long to answer, the interview is going to last six months.* A 'Sarah's wedding' reply would prompt me to ask only vital questions and to say that I have to be back at the office in an hour, whether it was true or not, so I'm afraid we'll have to hurry.

People take all kinds of diversions in an interview. It isn't easy to know whether you should drag them back. Letting them wander off might lead somewhere more interesting than the original topic. Or that ten-minute anecdote that began with them buying cat food might end with the realisation that buying cat food was the best bit.

Those who can't stop talking are preferable to those who barely start. To try and loosen up reticent interviewees I'd throw in a question or a comment that had nothing to do with the interview. I'd change my demeanour by becoming more formal or relaxed. My personality took a back seat. I became whoever I thought would extract the best answers.

I'd already have chosen my accent so that it bore some resemblance to theirs, working on the theory that this would create a degree of empathy. I spoke Cumbrian like the native I was. My version of a neutral middle-class accent was passable. And when interviewing anyone aristocratic I'd hear myself turning into Prince Charles.

Being a chameleon could lead to awkward situations. For one

feature I acted as landlord for a day at a Carlisle pub. The job had been arranged over the phone with a brewery company PR man called Simon. He was quite posh so instead of saying 'sure' I said 'shore', and other such betrayals of my working-class origins.

This pub had a rough reputation. I greeted the landlord and his regulars with the Carlisle accent I'd grown up with. The Carlisle accent is not a graceful thing. It's a verbal mugging: an ugly mongrel of Geordie, Scottish and Martian. Conversation between Cumbrians and the rest of the galaxy can be challenging. A colleague told me about a friend from the south who visited a Whitehaven café and asked for a latte. The waitress brought them a cup of tea.

'Sorry – what's this?'

'It's your la'al tea.'

La'al is Cumbrian dialect for little.

A similar communication breakdown loomed in the pub. I'd been talking to everyone there like Nora Batty's son. That was fine until, unexpectedly, Simon walked in. Bollocks. From the way I'd spoken on the phone, he'd have been expecting to meet someone who owned the Lake District. For the next few hours I tried to talk to him only in quiet corners – 'Shore, Simon, shore' – while continuing to converse in deepest Cumbrian with my new drinking buddies.

***

Before interviewing someone for a profile, I did as much research as time allowed and printed a list of questions, largely as a safety net if I couldn't think what to ask next. I kept it close because I didn't want the interviewee to see what was on it, in case they thought I was following a script – which I was, to an extent – and in case any questions were controversial.

It was wise to save these until the end of the interview. That way, if 'Is it true about you and the sheep?' prompted a walkout, you'd have other things to write about. Although who'd want to read about anything other than the walkout and the sheep?

There were several interviews with an elephant, or a sheep, in the room. The whole time I'd be thinking, *I'll have to ask about the sheep soon*, while they were probably thinking, *When's he going to mention the sheep?*

One example was mountaineer Simon Yates. In 1985 Yates and Joe Simpson had climbed in the Andes. Their descent went badly wrong. Simpson fell and broke his right leg. For the next few hours they were roped together while Yates lowered Simpson, then realised that he'd lowered him over a cliff. Simpson's weight was dragging them off the mountain. Yates was faced with a choice: he and Simpson fall to their deaths, or he cuts the rope and saves himself.

He cut the rope. Days later Yates was about to leave base camp when Simpson appeared, having somehow survived the fall and dragged himself five miles. This ordeal inspired Simpson's best-selling book, *Touching the Void*.

My interview with Yates was arranged to talk about his new book. It had occurred to me that he might be touchy about *Touching the Void*. Simpson was the miracle survivor who crawled to safety with a broken leg. Yates was the man who cut the rope. I'd read that some people thought he shouldn't have done it, as if they would happily plunge to their death as long as they were doing it with a friend.

For half an hour we talked about Yates's book while I wondered how to mention *Touching the Void*. It seemed unfair to ambush him many years after the event. But I wouldn't have interviewed Neil Armstrong without asking about the moon. I tried to edge him towards it with questions about fear and danger. It didn't work. Having failed to get there organically, eventually I blurted 'So, *Touching the Void . . .*' Here's how I described his reaction.

> Instantly there's a change in Yates. It's like I've flicked a switch. One that operates a freezer. He stiffens in his seat and his face becomes expressionless. I feel as if I've betrayed him. I came here to talk about his new book but in the end I'm just like every other journalist, wanting my own crack at you-know-what.

I asked him a series of questions that must have become cruelly familiar over the years. His answers were abrupt. I changed the subject and a bit of warmth returned. If I demonstrated any imagination in this interview it was at the end, when I asked Yates about what happened when I mentioned *Touching the Void*. Why did he become like a different person?

He said he gets asked the same questions over and over again, and that the only good ones came from schoolchildren. 'They say things like "Were you frightened?" It's such an obvious question. And yet all these dozens of journalists have not asked a really good question. "Were you frightened?" Obviously the answer is "Yes, I was very frightened."'

So was I. But raising an awkward subject was less nerve-wracking than explaining to an editor why I hadn't asked the question that readers wanted answered.

I was relieved that Yates didn't ask to see my feature before it was published. That happened maybe one interview in ten, and could sour a pleasant encounter. Normally it was a tentative, 'Will I be able to have a look at this before it goes in the paper?' At the other end of the scale was 'I'll need you to send me this to make sure I'm happy with it.'

I'd explain that we didn't show people stories before publication unless it was an advertising feature that they were paying for. Sometimes I dared to say that there had to be an element of trust, while wondering if asking people to trust a journalist was a good tactic. I'd say, 'We'd never get a paper out if everything we wrote had to be vetted by everyone we spoke to. But if there's anything you're worried about, just let me know and I'll try to reassure you.' That usually did the trick. No one ever said, 'In that case, stick it up your arse,' although a few were probably tempted.

There were exceptions to all this. If it was a sensitive subject such as abuse or illness, I'd agree that they could see it. If it was something very technical such as an interview with a scientist, I'd ask if I could send them certain sections to check.

I once interviewed CN Group's chief executive. He didn't interfere in the editorial process, which we appreciated. But perhaps this meant he wasn't familiar with post-interview protocol. Afterwards he rang me and asked to check the feature. I asked a senior member of the team what to do. They shrugged and said, 'It's his paper.' I sent him the interview. He responded with a phone call requesting a couple of, thankfully minor, changes.

Some interviews went to an unexpected place. The interviewee was telling me about a tragedy I'd been unaware of. Perhaps a loved one had died. And as they talked, part of me was thinking, *This is good . . .* My story would raise awareness of the illness, or the dangerous junction, or whatever had caused the tragedy. Part of me, though, was pleased that what I was writing about had just become more interesting.

For a feature about homelessness I spoke to a man who was sleeping on the streets. It was November and cold. I arranged to meet him that night, at the bench where he said he'd be. He wasn't there. I wandered around Carlisle until 2 a.m. but didn't find him. Next day he was back at the bench. He explained that he'd slept on a friend's sofa. I was annoyed. How dare he find somewhere warm to sleep when he should have been showing me what it's like to be lonely and cold.

Shortly after starting at CN Group, I heard a story that sums up how being a good journalist doesn't always sit neatly with being a good human being. One morning, years earlier, news had come through of a fatal accident the previous night. A reporter had the victim's name. It was the same as a member of staff's. Was it the same woman?

After a few phone calls, and just before the deadline for the day's first edition, this was confirmed. The reporter solemnly told the news editor, 'I'm afraid it is our Susan.' (I've changed her name.) The news editor punched the air and said, 'Yes! We've got a picture of her!'

The person who told me this story seemed both appalled and amused by it. 'I've never seen anyone so jubilant about a colleague's death,' he said.

Sometimes I went too far in the opposite direction, too sensitive to push into uncomfortable territory. At an event to publicise a fire-service recruitment campaign I interviewed some firefighters. I asked one man why he'd joined the service. He said, 'My brother died in a car crash when I was sixteen. Something like that helped to spur me on to help people.'

Usually I would have asked more. What was his brother like? How close were they? How did he hear about his death? How did it affect him? Did he speak to any of the firefighters who rushed to the scene? Did he go to see his brother's body? Did he say anything to him, out loud or in his head, like a goodbye or a pledge to become a firefighter so that something good could come out of this tragedy?

I didn't ask any of those things. That day I couldn't face dredging up someone's pain. Maybe he'd have become upset. But maybe he wanted to talk about it, to pay tribute to his brother or to the firefighters. I'll never know, because I didn't do my job.

***

I'd flatter myself into thinking that I peeled away surface layers to reveal the person within. Occasionally, evidence arrived to show that I didn't know them at all.

For one colour piece I spent Friday night at a karaoke competition in a Carlisle bar. Its star was a nineteen-year-old who'd won several previous karaoke nights, and went on to win this one. He sang 'Poison' by Alice Cooper extremely well. He was a lot louder on stage than off it, and not just because of the microphone. He was polite, inquisitive and passionate about singing. He told me he'd recently been to Blackpool to see some agents.

Two months later he tried to lure an eight-year-old boy into a cubicle in a public toilet. He admitted the offence and was put on the sex offenders' register. Three years after his court appearance, he died of a drug overdose. His father told the inquest there had been previous overdoses. But he didn't think his son had wanted to die. The coroner recorded an open verdict.

All these stories were illustrated in our papers with a picture of him taken that karaoke night, scowling in ghoulish Alice Cooper-style make-up. I couldn't have known what was in his mind: those who shared his life remained oblivious. He offered them what interviewees generally offered me. His best side.

I interviewed a Scrabble player who the following year became UK champion. In hindsight, he gave some clues. There was a certain world-weariness and a comment that he didn't take the game very seriously. 'There's enough in life to depress me without a game of Scrabble doing it,' he said. He wouldn't elaborate, beyond describing himself as a cynic and saying, 'I don't hold humanity in particularly high regard.'

Five years after our interview she stepped on to a rail line and was killed by a train. She, because by now she was transgender. She'd told a psychiatric nurse that she felt stigmatised because of this and was being taunted in the street. I tried not to think about how that must have felt.

For more than fifty years the public face of our papers was Billy Dixon. This newspaper seller had the prime pitch in Carlisle city centre and was known by every local for his shout of 'Not many left!' in the days when we sold so many copies that his claim might even have been true. In 2002, at the age of eighty-one, he was jailed for historical sex offences. The man selling our papers was himself one of the biggest stories in Cumbria, hiding in plain sight.

We reported it, of course. A staff member who appeared in court could look forward to extensive coverage, to ensure we couldn't be accused of one rule for our employees and another for everyone else.

Elsie Baty had nothing to hide. But something sadly unexpected happened after our interview. Elsie had spent decades campaigning on behalf of residents in Carlisle's Botcherby estate. I interviewed her one Friday afternoon, having heard good things about her for years. At eighty-two she still fizzed with energy and righteous indignation, in this case over the removal of play-park equipment by the city council. 'Does anybody consult anybody or do they just do what they like?' she said. 'Is Botcherby too ignorant to be consulted?'

Three days later, Elsie died suddenly at home. One friend said, 'Ten women could not replace her. I've never met anyone like her before and it was a privilege to know her.'

After that, anyone I'd ever interviewed who died was used as evidence of 'The Curse of Lytollis'. If they were 112 and I'd talked to them ten years earlier, that didn't absolve me of blame.

7

Colour Schemes

I'D learned that features could be unpredictable and that something unexpected, such as a spectator fighting with a player on a football pitch, might make a colour piece more interesting. But some things were too interesting to publish.

One Sunday afternoon I spent a couple of hours in a Carlisle park with a twelfth-century battle re-enactment group. They were very pleasant people, despite devoting their weekends to attacking each other with swords, knives and arrows. Maybe working off aggression this way helps to explain why they were so nice.

I joined several warriors kneeling on the grass behind shields as others launched arrows at us. From perhaps fifty yards behind me I heard a boy's voice. I couldn't make out what he was saying. The voice became closer and louder.

'ARE YOU GETTING FUCKED UP THE ARSE?'

I turned around. Four boys, aged between about seven and thirteen, were approaching. The one who was asking the question – the oldest one – seemed to be reading too much into our kneeling position.

The frustrating thing about writing for a 'family newspaper' is that you can't always tell the full story. Instead of reporting what was said, I settled for 'They were cheeky, to put it mildly.'

The boys went on to pick up weapons, swear a bit more, and be generally obnoxious. The weekend warriors remained polite as they tried, with little success, to placate these intruders. Part of me was amused to see the warriors rendered powerless by a bunch of meddling kids. A much bigger part wanted them to attack the boys with their swords. Just the wooden ones though. They probably wouldn't have hurt all that much.

I wrote, 'If this really was the twelfth century, Carlisle's warriors would have all manner of ways to dispel their tormentors. In the twenty-first, they were obliged to wait until they became bored and wandered off.'

Colour pieces often involve reporting on a group activity. I've written them about everything from foxhunting to trainspotting. Arriving at any such gathering was daunting, knowing that I'd have to make sense of what seemed like chaos. Describing what happened and capturing the atmosphere usually turned out to be straightforward enough. But there was the knowledge that I couldn't interview everyone – that someone might have an amazing story and the odds were against me finding them. The journalist is playing God in deciding who to speak to, as well as in the usual ways of what to ask them and how to write it.

The Grumpy Old Git Club – a group of retirees who met every week – presented the challenge of a dozen men talking, often over each other, about everything from airport parking to koi carp. The group's name seemed misleading. 'I had to be honest with David: I liked him and his colleagues, but they didn't seem grumpy at all. "When we're grumpy we get really grumpy," he insisted. "You've caught us on a bad day."'

Many colour pieces have a first-person element. The journalist takes part in an activity and explains what it's like. I was Cumbria's answer to John Noakes, trying things that often involved falling over and generally being out of my depth.

One example was Uppies and Downies: the centuries-old mass

participation football game played on the streets of Workington at Easter. That wasn't supposed to be a first-person piece. But the photographer decided that me in the middle of the scrum of hulking blokes would make a good picture. He shoved me in, I looked scared, and everyone was happy.

The week before it officially opened, I spent five days walking Hadrian's Wall Path from Wallsend, on Tyneside, to Bowness-on-Solway in Cumbria. Demonstrating the kind of common sense that characterised my career, I bought new boots the day before embarking on this cross-country trek. After five miles my feet were blistered and bleeding. Never mind – only seventy-nine miles to go. The morning after I'd limped into Cumbria, we received complaints about a picture on the *News & Star*'s front page. My shredded feet put people off their Shredded Wheat.

When *Strictly Come Dancing* started, I took part in a ballroom dancing class. I'd dreaded being photographed dancing. Even worse was the prospect of being photographed without a partner. The instructor said he would find me one. He asked a woman if she wanted to dance with me. Her response suggested he'd asked if she fancied dental surgery with no anaesthetic. 'Michael approached another woman. She gave a similar reaction. I was about to start tunnelling through the floor with my hands.'

A Cumberland Wrestling demonstration in the centre of Carlisle was particularly mortifying. Competitors in this traditional sport wear vests, long johns and shorts. I used to think this looked a bit silly. But it looked as normal as a jumper and jeans compared with the pimped-up version I borrowed from a champion wrestler.

The funny thing about wearing turquoise shorts adorned with embroidered flowers and a vest with a parrot and a carrot sewn on is that, when you put them on, you feel even more embarrassed than you thought you would. But I couldn't say anything. This was traditional costume. Criticising it would have been blasphemy, like turning up at Old Trafford and saying 'I'm not sure about all this red.'

I've heard of people having disastrous holidays because their tattoos happen to match those of a local gang. Wearing the outfit of a champion wrestler when you are not a champion wrestler felt similar to that. I tried to explain to the proper wrestlers that I'd never done this before. Some seemed reluctant to believe me. Who would wear such an ostentatious outfit if they hadn't earned the right?

The event took place outside the town hall. Before my first bout, one wrestler was badly hurt when thrown to the ground. I saw him carried into an ambulance. He'd broken his collarbone. That didn't do a lot for my nerves. But his absence meant that I was drafted in to more bouts than originally planned. I had the shit beaten out of me by every wrestler in Cumbria. Some respected my novice status and pulverised me gently. Others just picked me up and hurled me down. In one such encounter I landed on the big toe of my right foot. It hurt for months and still clicks in cold weather.

Not every activity was so frantic, such as a game of darts against former world champion Eric Bristow. I didn't make a great start. It took me five minutes just to get the flights in my darts. By then, Eric had worked himself into a competitive frenzy. 'All right, son? Take your time. If you're nervous, have a couple of pints.' That was my kind of sport.

A feature on wild swimming began with a morning dip in Crummock Water. It was July. But this was Cumbria. 'Raw cold shreds my nerve ends. I'm gasping and shouting wordless noise. So cold it's painful, right down through my body. I feel like the colour blue.' I keep hoping Cumbria Tourism will quote those words on its posters. Once I'd warmed up – kind of – it became exhilarating, the kind of job where you can't quite believe you're being paid to do this.

I've seen features described as 'the story behind the story'. Lots of my ideas for colour pieces came from reading a news story and thinking there was more to be said about the people involved.

Reports of assaults on hospital staff led to me spending a Saturday night in the Cumberland Infirmary's accident and emergency unit. No staff were attacked. But they dealt with the effects of other violence. A nurse told me that more than half of Saturday-night admissions were alcohol related: people injured in fights and people falling over. I saw numerous examples of both. A man with a broken jaw kept wandering off as staff tried to X-ray him. Other patients had been headbutted and bottled.

Before long the number of young men arriving with blood pouring from head wounds became monotonous. Someone rang for information about an assault victim. 'You'll have to be more specific,' one of the nurses told them. 'We've had about nine assaults in here tonight.' No wonder the nurse told me they prayed for rain on Saturday nights.

From a cubicle I heard young women laughing. They were friends of a woman who had collapsed after drinking too much. Next door an elderly woman who'd fallen out of bed cried in pain with a broken arm.

One night I reported on a fire service road-safety campaign. This included firefighters cutting a volunteer out of a car. I arrived to find that my editor had volunteered me. My mock rescue was streamed live on Facebook. I saw later that viewers had posted comments such as 'Great to see the valuable work of our firefighters!' and 'Saving lives every day – well done guys!' A colleague told me that his wife had physically restrained him from posting the words 'Let him die.'

Another colour piece was supposed to look at the life of trawler fishermen in the Irish Sea. They face all kinds of issues, I expect. The only issue that my feature explored was seasickness.

I'd arranged to meet a trawlerman at 5.30 one morning in early January. Getting up at 3.30 during the first week of the year was not an appealing prospect. It made this one of those jobs that felt as if it lasted much longer than the hours I was paid for. To me it began as soon as I got home from work the previous evening and realised I'd have to go to bed at 7.30 to have a chance of eight hours' sleep. I hardly slept at all for fear of not waking in time. I arrived exhausted and feeling as if I'd already put in a twelve-hour shift.

I'd worried about seasickness. As the trawler set off, I felt fine. When it left the shelter of the harbour, things changed. I was drinking coffee on deck. The sea was fairly calm but the boat began to bounce. Everything smelt of fish: who knew?

The radio was playing 'Bohemian Rhapsody'. When I hear the song now, it sparks a memory of hanging over the side and throwing up my breakfast. The trawlerman suggested that I go down to his cabin and rest. For the next few hours all I saw was wood-panelled walls and the insides of my eyelids.

My colour piece turned out to be monochrome. I wrote it based around a phone interview with the trawlerman the next day, sprinkled with what little atmosphere I'd gleaned from my few minutes above deck.

The photographer who accompanied me wasn't seasick. He had a lovely time, a highlight of which was his photo of me vomiting.

And he found another way to relieve me of my dignity. For the next couple of days, people in the newsroom looked at me with even more suspicion than usual. Then someone came out with a question I'd never expected to hear.

'Did you really have a dump on the deck of that trawler?'

Journalism lecturers are now using this as an example of fake news. The answer to the question was 'No.' I'd briefly surfaced from my sickbed to ask the trawlerman where the toilet was. He laughed and handed me a bucket. The photographer, for his own amusement, had reported what happened next without mentioning one important detail: the bucket. Predictably, many people preferred to believe his version. I soon learned that that's the kind of claim you can't deny very strongly before it sounds as if you're protesting too much.

That wasn't the only time I felt guilty for writing about something without experiencing it myself. In 2000 David Beckham made headlines after paying £300 for a number two (very short) haircut. I was sent to a traditional barber to see what he thought about it. George Johnstone charged just £3.50 for the same cut. 'If you paid me three hundred pounds, I'd take all day,' he said. One of his customers added, 'For three hundred pounds I'd be wanting a car.'

I had considered letting George give me a number two for the sake of the feature, but decided that would be a step too far. Next day I felt as if I'd let myself down by losing my nerve. So I bought some clippers and cut my own hair at home. The result was horribly uneven and brutally ugly. I was struggling with depression at the time. My hair looked, and felt, like self-harm.

First thing next morning I called into a barber near work and asked if he could salvage my DIY nightmare. All he could do was shave my head, so short that he removed the guard from the clippers. When he'd finished, I made Beckham's number two look like a hippy wig.

I wore a hat as I walked into the newsroom, taking it off only when I'd sat down. The laughter started within seconds. Colleagues crowded around to stare. People elsewhere in the building were summoned for a look. It was actually enjoyable. I loved making people laugh and didn't always care if it was with me or at me. A sub-editor persuaded me to have my picture taken and used it on the Beckham haircut feature. 'I'll only use it small,' he lied.

8

Crossing the Border

A FEW weeks later I began seeing someone who lived in Edinburgh. Before long I'd fallen in love with her and the city. Over the next few months, we discussed the possibility of me moving up there. I'd wondered if I could make it on a bigger paper. The *Edinburgh Evening News* was selling 70,000 copies a day. That was nearly three times the *News & Star*'s circulation and nearly double that of the *Cumberland News*. Then there was the prestige of working for a capital city's newspaper.

Early in 2001, I spoke to someone in the *Evening News*'s features department and an interview with the editor was arranged. The *News* was a sister title of the *Scotsman*. Both papers' HQ was a new stone and glass building with views to the craggy hills of Holyrood Park, around the corner from where the new Scottish Parliament would soon be opening. The spectacular environment heightened my ambition. I wanted to prove I was good enough to work somewhere like this.

The interview seemed to go well. A few days later I received a letter offering me a job. Although there was no doubt that I'd accept it, I was sad to be leaving Cumbria. Most of my friends and family were there. I loved my job. But Edinburgh was a challenge. And journalism had taught me not to run from those.

My leaving presentation took place in the newsroom on my last afternoon. Everyone knew that someone as quiet and quietly spoken as me would be dreading speaking in front of dozens of people. Keith Sutton walked in, carrying something hidden under a blanket. The big reveal: it was a microphone. There was no need for it because I had my own surprise. I'd asked a sub to print some bills, which I held up.

Thank you.
It's been a pleasure.
Goodbye.

***

My first day at the *Edinburgh Evening News* felt like starting again. Who are these people? Where's Haddington? Where, for that matter, are the toilets? I was introduced, briefly, to my new colleagues by the features editor. Briefly, because I was sent out on a job within minutes of arriving. The *News* was like that.

Scotland's newspaper market was fiercely competitive. At CN Group my main competition had been BBC Cumbria and ITV Border. Now it was local and national TV and radio, plus every national paper. Each English national had a Scottish edition that included Edinburgh news. There were also three homegrown nationals: the *Daily Record*, the *Scotsman* and the *Herald*. The *Scotsman* was a rival of the *Evening News* as well as its stablemate.

The *News* was an excellent paper and standards were high. The price was a lot of stress on its staff. The editor, John McLellan, was an intense Scot who stalked the newsroom every morning as that day's edition was finalised.

Features were an important part of the *News*'s arsenal. I was one of four full-time feature writers. Most of our work was for a daily features supplement called 'Capital City'. The pace was fast, and life was made harder by my lack of local knowledge. I was like the journalists I'd seen in Cumbria who had moved to the area from elsewhere. How could they not know where Brampton is? Now I was like that with Haddington. And Ingliston. And the toilets.

I'd always taken for granted my ability to put stories in context. That became harder now. *This thing I'm writing about: is it unusual for Edinburgh? Do I need to spell out the background or will readers already know? If I do need to spell out the background, what is the background?*

Most difficult of all was knowing who to speak to. In Cumbria, whatever the story, I would either know who to contact or I'd know who to ask to find out. The only person I knew in Edinburgh was my girlfriend. That was handy for stories about student nurses and Smirnoff Ice. Sadly the *News* didn't carry very many of those.

A problem facing all feature writers was the way the paper was organised. Some features were planned well in advance, but by no means all. There was a daily conference for department heads. The features editor would emerge at 11 a.m. or later with instructions for one or two of us to produce spreads for the following day's paper, usually about something topical. Our deadline was 4 p.m. The chosen ones had a maximum of five hours, minus any lunch break, to research the subject, work out who to speak to (this often needed to be several people), track them down, interview them and write 1,200 words.

Making sure the paper had topical stories was fair enough, unless it was me who had to write them. In that case I'd have been happy for us to focus on Elizabethan architecture and Bronze Age trading routes.

When the features editor approached my desk after a conference, the *Mission: Impossible* theme tune began playing in my head. 'Roger – I need a spread for tomorrow's paper on Edinburgh folk who play underwater tennis. We're only interested in female players, between the ages of twenty-six and twenty-eight-and-a-half. Just those whose first name begins with a consonant and whose surname ends with a vowel. Oh, and they need to be triplets. Speak to all three, please.'

OK, it wasn't quite that bad. I just didn't enjoy jobs that relied more on my contacts book than my writing, and which began with the stomach-churning thought, *How the hell am I going to do this?* Make lots of phone calls was the inevitable answer.

Still, I threw myself into the job. And when I was able to venture outside it was hugely enjoyable. Highlights included a colour piece about Edinburgh's under-fire traffic wardens. I persuaded the city council to let me spend a few hours with a warden and attend a morning briefing. The council may have regretted this when my feature was published: 'A checklist on the wall reminds wardens of the equipment they need. The list ends with the words "Have A Nice Day!" Underneath, someone has scrawled: "F*** you too."'

In another colour piece I flew over the Forth road and rail bridges with a display pilot and experienced the terror as he rolled his tiny plane upside down. The breeze was frightening enough. 'Within a few seconds a gust of wind blew us to the left. Another threw us to the right. Every bit of turbulence felt like a hurricane. Someone farted in Dalkeith and we were sent spinning sideways.'

Just as nerve-wracking was reporting from an estate notorious for young people committing crimes, including a nine-year-old boy who'd been arrested more than forty times in the past year.

Since arriving in Edinburgh I'd been worried that people would have a go at me for being English. It had never happened. But I played up my northernness just in case, taking any opportunity to tell people that I was from Carlisle. 'It's less than ten miles from the border,' I'd say, as if this made me Oor Wullie.

On that estate I was convinced I'd be abused for being an English bastard criticising their home. But everyone I spoke to was friendly. Less so the two boys aged around ten who walked past and called the female photographer a fucking bitch.

This was very different to the part of Edinburgh in which I was renting an expensive shoebox. I'd seen the city as a film set. Impossibly pretty. Hard to believe that people lived here. And a few miles away were burned-out cars and children throwing stones at pensioners.

One of my favourite jobs was an interview with Irish comedian Dave Allen. When growing up I'd been allowed to stay up late and watch his shows. It turned out he had a passion for painting, and his first exhibition was about to open in Edinburgh. It was only a phone interview, but he was funny and kind, just as I'd hoped.

He said he'd tried to paint in summer meadows, which hadn't worked out as planned: 'The canvas just got covered with fucking flies. It became a graveyard for dead creatures with their legs stuck in the paint. Still, it did give a bit of body to the painting.'

His most recent TV series had been three years earlier. I asked if he was planning any more. 'I'm relaxing in my later years. You spend all your life working to reach a point where you don't have to work. When you reach that point, people say "Why aren't you working?"'

I thanked him for the interview and gushed that I was a big fan. He said he hoped that he'd given me an insight into the man I'd known only on screen. As far as I can tell, that was his last interview. There were no more TV series. He died four years later. The Curse of Lytollis.

The pressure for good stories wasn't pretty. I interviewed a ninety-four-year-old who had spent three years as a prisoner of the

Japanese during the Second World War. He'd been punched and kicked in the head and saw comrades beaten to death. One of my senior colleagues thought this wasn't sufficiently dramatic. Hadn't he been tortured? I said no: I'd methodically asked him about what he'd been through. Being viciously beaten and watching friends die was the worst of it.

'Can you ring him and check?'

I didn't argue strongly enough. I could even have pretended to ring him without doing so. But I did ring him. I apologised for calling and asked if he could confirm that the worst thing that had happened to him had been the beatings. He said yes. I thanked him, and broke the news to my disgruntled colleague that this chap had not been tortured.

***

On the last day of the 1998–9 season, Carlisle United were about to be relegated from the Football League after seventy-one years. To avoid plunging into non-league oblivion, which may well have killed the club, they had to win their final match, at home to Plymouth Argyle. With one second remaining, the score was 1–1. Then Carlisle scored the winning goal. The scorer was their goalkeeper. Jimmy Glass had run the length of the pitch to join the attack. The ball fell at his feet and he belted it into the net.

The story made headlines around the world. The goal went on to be ranked seventh in *The Times*'s list of the most important goals in football history. I interviewed Jimmy several times and we got on well. A couple of years later he rang me and said he wanted to write his autobiography. Well, he wanted to talk and he wanted me to do the writing. I was flattered and gladly agreed.

We began working on the book just before my move to Edinburgh and continued over the next few months. I was interviewing Jimmy on the phone at night and occasionally in person, as well as writing up these interviews and researching his career. Edinburgh had been my favourite city. Now it felt hard to appreciate. I'd come home feeling drained, then work on the book and go to bed. I was too tired and stressed to give much attention to my girlfriend. I could feel us moving apart.

One afternoon in the newsroom I noticed people gathered around a TV. Someone told me that a plane had flown into the World Trade Center. Just then, another plane drifted into shot and hit the second tower. For the next few days, 9/11 was all I watched or read about. It compounded my feeling of unease. Something about it made me want to get home, to Cumbria.

I felt I was struggling at work. There were too many underwater-tennis triplets to track down. Not enough of the colour pieces and profiles that were my strength. I told the features editor I was thinking of leaving. She asked me not to. My girlfriend reacted in the same way. 'If you leave, what will you do?' I didn't know. But a week later I wrote a letter to John McLellan, waited until he was out, and left it on his desk. The letter thanked him for giving me a job and said I was handing in my notice. I can't remember if I gave a reason.

He never spoke to me again. The features editor didn't say much. No one did. This was a high-pressure environment and I couldn't hack it. Survival of the fittest. Leave the weak ones and move on.

In hindsight, I can see that the depression that had plagued me for much of my life had taken control. Throughout school and university there were spells when I felt empty and alone with no solution in sight. Here was another. Things got tough and I didn't have the resilience to cope. A difficult few weeks culminated in me throwing away the years of work I'd put in to reach the *Evening News*.

There was no leaving presentation. That would have been embarrassing for everyone, just five months after I'd arrived. My leaving do consisted of a few pints with the deputy business editor, while wondering what happens next.

My plan had been to freelance. But that required a lot more energy and confidence than I was feeling. The next couple of weeks were like a holiday, spending more time with my girlfriend and enjoying Edinburgh. Then the monthly bills and my non-existent salary highlighted the cost of our city-centre shoebox. My resignation had destroyed any prospect of another journalism job in Edinburgh, and in most places. The only place I might have a chance was Cumbria. Returning so soon would be humiliating, but a lot better than not being a journalist.

I emailed the deputy editor in Carlisle and explained my situation. If any feature-writing jobs came up, would he bear me in mind? He said he'd have me back immediately. This was November. I arranged to return at the beginning of January. Now I had to tell my girlfriend. She was upset that I was abandoning her, and that I hadn't discussed going back to Cumbria, other than as a vague possibility. The next few weeks were strained. I worked on the Jimmy Glass book and tried to block out the recent past and the immediate future.

***

I was in denial about leaving Edinburgh. Three days before returning to Carlisle, I had nowhere to live there. I contacted a friend from work and arranged to move into his spare room. The previous April I'd been a bright young thing off to fulfil his potential. Now I skulked back as someone who had tried the big, wide world and come running home.

Most people were too tactful to do anything other than welcome me. The old-school news editor muttered that I shouldn't have come back. He was disappointed. He'd had high hopes for me. On the plus side, I was reminded that working for a smaller paper could mean writing better stories. Not long after my return I profiled Britain's oldest professional boxer, having travelled with him to a fight. That's the kind of feature I love to write, and read, where a hidden world is revealed. I'd suggested something similar in Edinburgh and been told it would be too time-consuming.

Work was a distraction from the fact that my relationship was hanging by a thread. The life I'd left behind, and how I'd messed it up, haunted me. I visited a doctor and agreed to take antidepressants. They'd been suggested before. Now I couldn't see another way through the gloom.

After a few weeks, the drugs began taking effect. I felt a lot better. Then my girlfriend ended our relationship. I couldn't blame her after I'd left her in Edinburgh. That it seemed like my doing made the pain even worse. Being a journalist plugged the holes in my self-esteem. Rejection tore them open. How can someone love you and then not love you? In my job I'd asked thousands of questions. That was the one I really wanted an answer to.

I'd been for a meeting in London to discuss the Jimmy Glass book with one of the UK's biggest publishers. They emailed to say they'd decided against it. All that work, which had contributed to the demise of my relationship, looked like being for nothing. One morning soon after that I couldn't get out of bed, and I didn't care. I emailed the deputy editor and told him I was ill. For two weeks I hardly left my room.

On my first day back at work I had to fill in a form giving the reason for my absence. I was too embarrassed to mention depression, thinking word would spread, people would mock me, and the stigma would harm my career. I told the deputy editor the truth. He was understanding and we agreed to fudge the explanation.

It took a long time to get over my relationship failing. For months it was an open wound. There were frequent periods of not knowing how to get through the day. I never discussed my struggles with anyone at work. They felt like something to be ashamed of. So did my time in Edinburgh. I cringed when it was mentioned. If anyone asked how long I'd worked there, those five months became 'about a year'.

Life got slowly better, although over the next few years there were other periods of depression. Antidepressants helped, then exercise took over. To boost my mood naturally I trained at a gym and ran. Journalism was my real saviour: being forced into social situations and making a living from the one thing I thought I was good at.

The book was eventually published in 2004. Such was the ongoing fascination with Jimmy's goal that it received lots of publicity in national and local media.

Seven years after the *Kilroy* debacle came my second TV appearance, talking about the book with Jimmy. It turned out that my fear of not selling any books outweighs my fear of public speaking. This was only on ITV Border but it was still a scary prospect. While preparing to record the interview at the station's studio, in the corner of my eye I noticed something moving. I glanced up just in time to see a light toppling over before it landed on my head, which left me dazed, and undoubtedly improved my interview.

9

Jordan, Boris, Strippers and Booze

By the time I became a journalist, the legendary days of liquid lunches had gone. But reporters, feature writers, photographers and subs would often go out together after work. Occasionally I'd stagger into the newsroom the morning after a session to be tasked with writing a piece about the evils of binge drinking.

I stopped drinking on work nights after interviewing one of Cumbria Police's most senior officers. I was hungover but managed to struggle through. We spent the interview sitting opposite each other with no desk between us. At the end as we stood to shake hands, I thought, *That went well*. Leaving the room, I saw that my fly was wide open.

In one way, alcohol made work easier. Any job that involved drinkers had an instant advantage. Their lack of inhibitions tended to spice things up.

In 2003 Katie Price, who was still known as Jordan then, appeared at a Carlisle club one Friday night. I was asked to interview her. It was a raucous event. She didn't arrive until eleven, giving those present plenty of time to drink. This included me. I always tried to be professional. But there comes a point when you look around and think, *Fuck it*.

The place was packed with more than a thousand plastered people. I was in the VIP section: some seats in a raised area with a bit of rope strung across the entrance. We VIPs had free drinks. There was a long time to wait and I was nervous. So I spent a couple of hours downing bottles of lager.

When Jordan arrived, the place erupted. 'Get your tits out for the lads!' was one of the politer chants. There was a Q&A. Someone asked if she was a lesbian. Gulp. The bar for the standard of questions had been set intimidatingly high.

I was given a few minutes with her and she was very pleasant. My last question made the lesbian query seem like something from David Frost's interview with Richard Nixon.

'What size are your breasts?'

In my defence, this was a major national talking point in 2003. She said, 'They're 32DD.'

'Don't the papers say they're bigger than that?'

'I don't read what the papers say. I just look at the pictures.'

At the end of the interview our photographer stepped forward. 'Would you like me to sit on your lap?' said Jordan. Of course I would. All my friends would see the picture. It would be great. She perched on my lap. The camera clicked. Happy days.

I hung around until Jordan left then I staggered to the office. It was 3 a.m. by now. I rattled off three hundred words for that day's *News & Star*. As had been the case all night, adrenalin seemed to cancel out the alcohol. I like to think that my intro captured the majesty of the occasion. 'Britain's most famous breasts were hanging out in Carlisle last night.'

A few hours later I bought the paper, eager to see myself with one of the most famous people in the country. The story was on page three, naturally. The main picture was Jordan on my lap. Oh no. She looked great. I looked terrified. The fear I'd felt was etched in my face. It was the fear of knowing that hundreds of people were staring at me. I'd tried to look cool but my eyes were wide in a way that betrayed my discomfort. No one said a word about what I'd written. All anyone mentioned was how scared I looked. The phrase 'rabbit in the headlights' was particularly popular. I wondered if my fear in social situations was always this visible.

Earlier I mentioned spending a day as the landlord of a Carlisle pub. The brewery that owned the pub was trying to recruit managers. It thought that a journalist messing about in one of its hostelries might inspire people to give the industry a try. I'd never been in that pub before, largely thanks to its fearsome reputation. I hoped that any violent types would leave me alone because I was a journalist, while fearing that they'd attack me because I was a journalist.

I arrived at noon one Friday. The landlord offered me a pint. I explained that I was here to work: perhaps I'd have one at the end of the day, thank you. Eleven hours later I stumbled outside, having started drinking at 2 p.m.

I'd got all I needed for the feature very quickly. My day's work consisted of being shown around the pub, interviewing the landlord and a few customers, and pulling a pint very badly. Then I drank beer – free beer – for nine hours. I also played snooker, kind of. I was so drunk that I missed the cue ball when trying to break off. I had new sympathy for those landlords who struggle with the temptation to drink all day. At this rate I'd have been dead in a week.

One interview was with a chap called Gilbert. 'I had my first pint in here, in 1950,' he said. 'My dad brought me in when I was eighteen.' He took a sip of his latest pint and added, 'I've seen a goat in here.' I wish everyone told me that they'd seen a goat in the place where I interviewed them. It would make my features a hell of a lot better.

The customers were friendly. But my anxiety about being attacked returned when a notorious football hooligan walked in. During the 1990s he'd been described by the national tabloids as England's worst hooligan. Or the best, depending on how you look at it. Back then I'd written a column about him. I didn't have a go at him – I was far too cowardly for that. The column was about how the media can pretend to be appalled by someone while writing salaciously about them. I made sure there could be no room for confusion: I was *not* having a go at him.

Soon after I'd written the article, I was in a club when a man claiming to be a friend of his told me that the hooligan was 'after me'. I spent the next few months terrified. All these years later he either didn't recognise me or he didn't care. Maybe he'd had a bad press all along. Bloody journalists.

I profiled Carlisle drag artist Billie Raymond. Being a drag artist in Cumbria has never been an easy option. Billie told me that he used to apply his make-up at home and leave the house in dark glasses. He had plenty of good lines. 'I once emptied a room full of soldiers when I got my snake out. I thought "The country's in safe hands with this lot."'

As part of the profile, I attended a charity night Billie had organised at a local club. Much of what happened could not be reported in the *News & Star*. Even the *Daily Star* would have blushed. Entertainment for the well-oiled women-only audience included two strippers called John and Mike. I wrote, 'John was dressed as a policeman, for a short while.' One of the strippers wore a cloak. As he beckoned the women with a finger, several rushed forward, knelt in front of him, and disappeared under the fabric.

I talked to one of these men in the dressing room, in what

turned out to be an unusual interview. Before going on stage, he masturbated as he spoke to me. I don't think he found me particularly attractive. He was just putting a bit of life into his penis before putting it on show. As he talked, I nodded and said, 'Hmm' and 'Yeah' and 'That's right', as if everyone has a wank while I'm interviewing them.

It became difficult not to stare when, having aroused himself sufficiently, he produced a roll of thread and tied some around the base of his knob to maintain his semi-erect state. A few minutes later he shrieked in pain as a spurt of blood gushed from the end. That must be an occupational hazard in this line of work. I wonder if they warn about it in careers lessons.

One Friday night in 2005 Boris Johnson missed his train and found himself stranded in Carlisle. In his *Daily Telegraph* column not long afterwards, he recalled heading to the pub and being stunned by 'the astonishing quantities of alcohol that were being necked by the denizens of Carlisle'.

You have no idea how much the city swelled with pride on reading those words. 'Astonishing quantities'. Beat that, Newcastle and Glasgow! There was much more, such as 'the pavements were Jackson Pollocked with the results of eating a kebab on top of eight pints of lager'. In his column Boris used this experience to illustrate Britain's devotion to binge drinking.

My editor Keith Sutton was ready to be outraged at the suggestion that Carlisle city centre on a Friday night may be a less than sober place. I was about to point out that everyone I'd spoken to had not only agreed with Boris but felt flattered by his depiction. Then Keith said, 'Get yourself to Henley-on-Thames [Boris's constituency at the time] this weekend. See what it's like on a Friday night. I bet it's not just full of people sipping rosé.'

I'd been planning a trip with my girlfriend that weekend. Keith said that she could come to Henley with me. Anyone whose experience of the journalism industry began after the 2008 financial crisis may be surprised by this. But there was a time when a local paper would pay for train fares and a hotel for a Cumbrian journalist and their partner to wander around an Oxfordshire town in the hope of embarrassing Boris Johnson. It was certainly a long shot: is Boris Johnson capable of feeling embarrassment?

Henley's Friday night was much calmer than Carlisle's, which doesn't say a lot. I wondered if the hefty price of drinks might be a factor. Binge drinking would be replaced by binge sipping if we had to pay those prices in Cumbria.

But Keith Sutton was right. Not everyone in Henley was drinking rosé. My girlfriend returned from the Ladies and reported that a woman with a 'Happy 18th Birthday' balloon had been in there with three young men, all of them sniffing white powder off the tiles next to a sink.

In a café next morning I overheard a conversation between two women. Their difference of opinion would be echoed around the country when Boris Johnson became Prime Minister fourteen years later.

'I love Boris. I think he must be incredibly clever because nobody could be that stupid. He must put it on.'

'No, he is that stupid.'

Keith seemed happy with the feature. Two months later he was less pleased with my next alcohol-related story. The new licensing act was about to come into force, allowing pubs and clubs to serve booze beyond their current hours: in some cases around the clock. Tony Blair's government hoped this would encourage a more relaxed attitude to alcohol.

I rang Carlisle-based drug and alcohol support charity Cadas. Its director didn't think extending licensing hours would have the desired effect. He also told me that Cadas had been helping a ten-year-old who was addicted to alcopops. Shit – I seemed to have stumbled across a story. That can happen occasionally, even to a feature writer.

Keith decided we'd run this as part of a series of stories about boozy Britain. Next day, a Tuesday, I was called into the morning conference. I rarely attended these. They were mainly for department heads. Keith asked me to write a colour piece about binge drinking based on a night on Botchergate: Carlisle's most raucous street, which is lined with pubs and bars. Great. When did he want me to do it?

'Tonight.'

It seemed obvious that the time for a story like this was Friday or Saturday night. But no one else raised any concerns and I lacked the confidence to voice mine. On the plus side, Keith had the accounts department give me fifty quid for drinks.

Having mentioned this to a couple of colleagues, I hit town that night with about ten volunteers in tow. The fifty quid didn't last long. The only binge drinkers in the quiet city centre were us. As I'd thought, this story shouldn't be done on a Tuesday. But the prospect of going into the newsroom empty-handed next morning terrified me.

Then inspiration struck. We'd published numerous stories about bars running drinks promotions. If a customer ordered a spirit, staff invited them to buy a double for just 10p extra.

Super Size Me, the documentary in which filmmaker Morgan Spurlock spent a month eating only at McDonald's, had been released the previous year, 2004. Whenever Spurlock was asked if he'd like a 'Super Size' meal, he said yes. Why couldn't I do the same with alcohol? I'd start ordering spirits. When I was asked if I'd like a double for an extra 10p, I'd say yes. What did my colleagues think of this idea? They only seemed to hear 'ten-pence spirits'. And they were very much in favour.

We went to one of those bars. I ordered a gin and tonic and was asked if I'd like a double shot of gin for an extra 10p. 'Yes, please.' After that, my memory of the evening comes only in snapshots. There were more double gins, on top of the pints of beer I'd downed before my brainwave. I remember us dancing in a club, barely able to stand because we were laughing so much. Drink may also have been a factor. I remember walking home at 2 a.m. and vomiting in the street. Some of it landed on my shoes. I remember thinking what a nice detail that would be in the feature I'd write in a few hours' time.

I'd told the features editor that I might be in late. It was nearly noon when I stumbled in with the hangover from hell. She asked if everything had gone OK. I told her the feature would be slightly different to what had been discussed, but it would be fine. I wrote it around the *Super Size Me* angle. Bars are encouraging binge drinking by offering customers a second shot of spirits for just 10p. I took them up on their offer: here's what happened. I sent the story and waited for the praise to flow.

The features editor was appalled. How could one of her journalists get drunk on duty? How could I be so irresponsible? She said I was encouraging binge drinking. She spoke to Keith and he agreed not to run the feature. I was also given a verbal warning.

I maintained that I'd done the right thing. We ran countless stories about the evils of binge drinking. So why not run one about what it's actually like? The argument that I'd be encouraging it didn't ring true, unless readers revelled in the idea of spewing on their shoes and feeling like a corpse.

The following Monday's *News & Star* splashed on my story about the ten-year-old alcoholic. Next day, the *Daily Mirror*'s splash had the headline 'An alcopops addict . . . at 10'. The story, marked 'Exclusive', was about a child in Cumbria. It featured my quotes from the head of Cadas.

I'd been out of the office the previous day. The *Mirror* journalist had left a message for me. If I'd rung her back even after she'd run the story, I might have been able to get some money. But having been labelled irresponsible, the knowledge that one of my stories about drinking was good enough to be a national paper's splash was all I needed.

Keith Sutton retired a few weeks later. His successor, Neil Hodgkinson, moved from the *Yorkshire Evening Post*, a much bigger paper. Editors in big media groups saw independent and respected CN as a place where quality still mattered, with less emphasis on squeezing huge profits.

A long-serving staff member once told me that the company always appointed editors who were very different from their predecessor. Neil was much louder than Keith, often laughing. I was never sure if he was genuinely amused or just trying to keep up morale. That quality was very much needed in the face of the challenges that would soon confront the newspaper industry.

10

Theatre Wins the Lottery . . . Literally!

REMEMBER Winsford? That's not the title of an Alan Bennett play. The mislocation of Winsford, you may recall, was when I became aware of sub-editors' ability to be a force for evil.

CN Group had some superb subs. Anthony Ferguson, for example. A music shop was burgled one night. The stolen items included classical instruments. His headline: 'Orchestral removers in the dark'.

He, and many other subs, designed stories to look appealing. The headline on my profile of a champion Scrabble player was written in the game's tiles. My feature about Britain's oldest boxer used a picture of him shadow-boxing. The picture was cut out, meaning the background was digitally removed from his body. It was replaced by shadow. The headline used a military-style font, which said, 'Fighting the years'.

But that's enough praise. My relationship with subs was usually one of barely suppressed rage. Not all of them were gifted at designing, headline writing or much else that the job demanded. Cut-outs were one example. When done well they enhanced the look of a story massively. Done badly, it seemed a four-year-old had been let loose with blunt scissors. Bits of people's heads went missing. The area around someone's shoes would include chunks of pavement.

What really annoyed me about some subs was their approach to my precious words. I wrote a feature about how National

Lottery funding for the arts had been slashed since the days when Theatre by the Lake in Keswick was funded largely by a lottery grant. My piece included the line 'The days of theatres winning the lottery are over.' A sub changed it to 'The days of theatres literally winning the lottery are over.'

Theatres literally winning the lottery? I'm sad to say I never saw a theatre stroll to the nearest corner shop and buy a ticket.

In my Cumberland Wrestling feature, the sub changed the description of my shorts from green to turquoise. Such attention to detail didn't extend to them noticing that using a longer word meant the last word of the feature dropped off the page.

Worst of all was when I'd written too much to automatically fit the shape that the sub was working in and, instead of making it fit by altering the number of pictures or the size of the headline, they just chopped off my last few paragraphs.

I spent many nights inflicting imaginary violence on people who did this. Around the world all kinds of atrocities were happening. And my fury was reserved for those who deleted some words I'd written in a local paper. Such dedication to my craft. Such tragic lack of perspective.

I regularly emailed the numerous chief sub-editors we had over the years. In one email I declared, 'This is not subbing – it's sabotage.' None of them appeared to care. It was almost as if they thought I was some kind of prima donna wanker.

Mine was an impotent rage. Our computer systems made it hard to tell which sub had worked on which story. That's partly why I emailed the chief sub, although I'd probably have been too cowardly to approach the offending sub directly anyway.

Many of their changes weren't huge. In a way, that made them more annoying. Most people in the newsroom, subs included, were extremely busy. And a few had the time to go nit-picking through more than a thousand words, often not removing errors but inserting them. I felt some subs were trying to justify their existence. If they had an hour or so to spend on a feature, they'd better be seen to have done something to it.

In the newspaper hierarchy, subbing was seen as a step up from reporting. Subs were generally paid more than reporters and feature writers. This status was based on their position as the last line of defence against libels in writers' copy. I don't recall any sub ever riding to the rescue that way. But the possibility was a useful negotiating tool.

This chapter was originally much longer. I'd listed many more ways in which subs undermined my work. Then I realised that they were doing their best, that it's not really that important, and that I'd better be careful in case any of them write a book about their career and wonder whether to include my balls-ups.

11

Stupid Bloody Questions

IN the early noughties I read that a journalist at a function had been bemused by the number of people who thought he earned a fortune. Eventually he asked everyone present to guess his salary. The lowest estimate was double what he earned.

In the years since then, many journalists' wages have hardly changed. There's still a perception that the job is well paid. Some journalists on national papers get big money but not at local level. As for perks, the only one I regularly received was a free copy of the paper every day. Even that became increasingly meaningless as more of the content was given away online.

Occasionally press trips were offered: a few days' free holiday in exchange for writing something nice about the place. Foreign ones were rare and fiercely contested. I went on just one press trip, to Cornwall in April 2010. This was a lovely four days of cream teas, surfing, a visit to the Eden Project, excellent restaurants. It was partly to promote new flights from Manchester to Newquay.

On the final day I came down for breakfast to hear that volcanic ash from Iceland had grounded flights across Europe. The flight from Manchester to Newquay had taken thirty-seven minutes. Newquay to Manchester by minibus took eight-and-a-half hours.

Some people would regard being a minor local celebrity as a perk. This wasn't exactly being given the best tables in restaurants. It was strangers saying 'Are you Roger Lytollis?'; me saying 'Yes';

and them saying 'I read your column.' I'd blurt 'Thank you!' before realising that they hadn't expressed an opinion, which left me wondering whether they liked it or read it down the phone to deter cold callers.

I was invited to give talks to groups such as Women's Institutes. My shyness meant I politely declined. I did feel bad about depriving them of the 'Are you getting fucked up the arse?' story.

I took part in two charity football matches against actors from Channel 4 soap *Hollyoaks*. My team – made up of local TV, radio and newspaper journalists – was called the No Stars. Before the second of these games, when the announcer read my name he made a quip about 'rogering'. That set the tone for an afternoon in which I played badly enough to be substituted after fifteen minutes.

Some people think journalism is glamorous because it's a branch of the media, on the same tree as the celebrities we interview. I sometimes thought that myself. Then I remembered a Sunday when I visited my parents' house. I'd spent much of the previous week writing – crafting – a feature about old people in poverty. Heartbreaking tales of war veterans scared to turn the fire up. As I talked to my mother in the back garden, I saw something familiar on the rabbit hutch floor. My old people in poverty feature, soaked in rabbit piss. That seems rather quaint in this internet age. These days the equivalent would be a rabbit urinating on a laptop.

The best antidote for any journalist who feels that their job is glamorous, or that they are any kind of celebrity, is a vox pop. *Vox populi* is Latin for 'Voice of the people'. I used to think it meant 'No, I don't want to answer your stupid bloody question.'

You'll probably have seen vox pops in newspapers and magazines, under a title such as 'Your Views'. They feature photos of several people answering a topical question. Or, more likely, the only question the features editor could think of that morning as they juggled a hundred jobs.

Vox pops are a rite of passage for young journalists. You might want to interview the Prime Minister. But the first rung on this ladder is persuading some strangers to tell you whether they prefer *Coronation Street* or *EastEnders*.

Journalism students at CN Group on work experience, and people who were there on a few days' trial for a job, were normally sent to do a vox pop. Some left the office as potential stars and came back exposed. They hadn't spoken to enough people, or they hadn't taken a picture of everyone they'd spoken to. They couldn't hack it. People were turned down for jobs on that basis.

Vox pops weren't a rite of passage for me. When I started at CN they were done by reporters. Sending a feature writer to do a vox pop would have been like asking Van Gogh to creosote your fence.

No one ever said it to me, but being parachuted in as a feature writer may have upset those reporters who'd spent years wanting to do the job I strolled straight into. I was just relieved to avoid the treadmill of typical reporters' roles, such as council meetings, death knocks and – perhaps worst of all – vox pops.

A colleague did one in Workington, a town whose down-to-earth name reflects its traditional nature. He was asked to find six publishable answers to the question, 'Should the age of consent for gay sex be lowered?' For two hours he received verbal abuse, threats of physical abuse, and people walking away shaking their heads. Eventually he resorted to ringing the newsroom and asking for an alternative question, ideally along the lines of 'What's your favourite colour?'

Another reporter made a similar plea after struggling for answers to a question about the conflict in Gaza. My features editor had set that one. She refused to provide an alternative, then asked me whether I thought the Gaza question was reasonable.

Generations of politicians around the world had failed to solve the Gaza problem. It was perhaps optimistic to expect a local newspaper reporter to find half-a-dozen people wandering through Carlisle with cogent views on the matter. Then again, the reporter in question had recently annoyed me. 'Sounds fine to me,' I said.

What happened a few months later felt like vengeance from the journalism gods. Several reporters had left, which led to my fellow feature writers and I being drafted in to do vox pops. The prospect horrified me. It took me back to the fear I'd felt when starting out more than a decade earlier of approaching strangers for quotes. At least on most jobs there was an easily explainable reason, such as 'You're a lorry driver and I'm asking lorry drivers if they eat muesli.'

With vox pops there was no reason other than 'Tomorrow's *News & Star* has some empty space. Your opinion on something you don't care about would help me to fill it.' I'd done the odd vox pop before. But now it was every couple of weeks and I had to find twelve people: six each for two questions.

In the good old days, writers did voxes with photographers. Now we had to take the pictures ourselves. Persuading people to be photographed was the most difficult part of this miserable process. It was always raining. Or maybe I've just imagined that, because no mood is so sunny that it can't be drowned by a vox pop. Out I'd go, juggling a notebook, pen, camera, umbrella and heavy heart.

I felt like a contestant on *The Apprentice* trying to persuade passers-by to purchase a treacle and seaweed smoothie. Students were most open to answering. Middle-aged men were the least likely. They'd often keep walking without acknowledging my existence. I was embarrassed about approaching women. 'Hello. Will you tell me your name, your age and where you live? And can I take your photo?'

Some were understandably suspicious, asking me for ID. When colleagues were out doing vox pops, I occasionally heard the newsdesk taking calls from members of the public enquiring if the person who'd just approached them really worked for the paper. When I was out, I wouldn't be at all surprised if they'd received calls about the sweating imbecile who'd wanted to know their favourite Womble.

I wasn't exactly picky when it came to answers. One question was 'What's your favourite Christmas song?' A man ummed and ahhed. 'Does it have to be a pop song, or could it be a carol?' It could have been his family emitting farts in G major after too many Brussels sprouts, as long as it filled three lines in next day's paper.

If somebody struggled to articulate an answer, I'd gently guide them towards one. Some colleagues bundled them into a van and drove them towards one at 90 miles an hour. A reporter told me he'd suggested an answer to a confused elderly person, then quickly added, 'So that's what you think, is it? Yes? Good – thank you.' As he walked away, he heard his subject mutter, 'What the bloody hell was all that about?'

It was frustrating when someone agreed to do it, answered the question, then refused to have their picture taken. I'd say things like 'The picture will be really small – you'll hardly be able to see it.' I made it sound as if the entire newspaper would be printed on a postage stamp. I'd have said anything to chalk another person off my list. Others would talk for ages, answering the question really well. I'd take notes, then ask for their name.

'My name? No – I don't want to be in the paper.'

'*What?* You don't want to be in the paper? I told you I'm a journalist. I told you what I'm doing. I've just spent five minutes writing down everything you've said. And you don't want to be in the *fucking* paper?'

I don't think I ever said that out loud.

Some journalists actually enjoy vox pops. They'll grab everyone they see and persuade them to answer any question. Favourite sexual position, with the picture taken in that position? No problem. What made it harder for me was that I saw vox pops from the public's perspective. When someone said 'No, thanks' and kept walking, I'd think, *I don't blame you – I'd do the same.*

Most of my voxes brought me close to a miniature nervous breakdown. While explaining who I was and what this was about, I'd try to appear calm while thinking, *Please agree to this – please. I just want it to be over.* After a few rejections I'd dread approaching anybody else. Everyone seemed scary and unfriendly. *Why can't I do this? I've been a journalist for years and I can't even persuade anyone to tell me who they want to win* Strictly Come Dancing.

But I often managed to persuade people who'd been unsure. And when I returned to the newsroom, having somehow got a dozen strangers to answer a random question and have their photos taken, I felt more satisfaction than for most features I'd written.

Sometimes, though, I found it impossible. I became more sympathetic to reporters who'd struggled with difficult questions. Anything to do with sex or politics guaranteed an hour or so of misery. Politics prompted responses such as 'They're all fucking wankers – and you can quote me on that!'

'Will do – thanks very much.'

I was once tasked with asking about research that said having lots of sex keeps people young. This may have sounded fun and quirky to my features editor. I knew it wouldn't seem that way to those I stopped in the street. My apologetic demeanour just ramped up the seediness. I didn't approach any women with that one, for fear of being sprayed with something toxic. Even the vast majority of men refused to answer. Eventually I rang contacts who we already had pictures of.

Phoning contacts went against the company's policy of approaching new people. A useful by-product of vox pops was building a library of faces, which could prove handy if any of them were later in the news. But when it came to voxes, I'd always been cautious about talking to strangers. Right from the start I'd grabbed people I knew, or who I recognised as having answered a previous question. After that question about sex, I began ringing or emailing contacts much more often. Doing a vox pop without being rained on or told to sod off was living the dream.

I sometimes resorted to asking those who I was interviewing about something else. I hoped readers wouldn't notice that the person on the centre spread opening their heart about living with an incurable illness was also on page thirteen revealing whether they thought the UK would win this year's Eurovision Song Contest.

Most of us who did regular vox pops developed ways of cheating. One colleague always interviewed the same man and woman who worked in a Carlisle shop. Is there life on other planets? Will Andy Murray win Wimbledon? Will Andy Murray win Wimbledon on other planets? They were happy to give an opinion about anything, and appeared in our papers more than some of our writers. News editors ordered that they weren't to feature again – their frequent presence was making us a laughing stock. Next week they were back. My colleague was happy to take a bollocking rather than speak to strangers.

Some journalists did voxes without speaking to anybody. Their friends had agreed that a quote could be invented on their behalf, as long as it was nothing controversial and they weren't made to look silly. The temptation to quote a macho, rugby-playing friend saying that their favourite childhood toy was a Barbie doll was resisted. Even that joy wouldn't have been worth losing the chance to make vox pops easier.

When wandering off-duty through places where I often did voxes, their sullen ghosts drifted alongside me. Castle Street is one of Carlisle's most picturesque places, dominated by the city's cathedral. Not by its castle: that would be ridiculous. I regularly paced Castle Street during vox pops, hoping to be insulted and ignored by a better class of passer-by. Soon, I could never go there without flashbacks making it hard to enjoy the area any more. I'd fallen victim to post-traumatic vox disorder. Sadly, the initials PTVD mean this condition struggles to be taken as seriously as it deserves to be.

I did voxes for seven years until they were scrapped. The only good thing that came out of them for me was a brief relationship. Our first conversation was whether she'd be watching Prince William and Kate Middleton's wedding. A year later we bumped into each other and dated for a few months. At times I've wondered whether that relationship was worth all the hellish hours spent trudging cold, wet streets. If we'd spent the rest of our lives together – long lives, another half-century or so – in a state of utter bliss, it might have been. Maybe.

Many years earlier, before the *News & Star* ran a vox pop every day, a colleague was sent on one with a view to its findings forming the basis of a news story. The question was 'Should capital punishment be restored?' He walked 50 yards and spoke to four people. Two were in favour of capital punishment. One was against it. One was a 'don't know'. This didn't have quite the scale or rigour of a YouGov poll. So my colleague was surprised to open next day's paper and see his story prominently displayed with the headline 'Bring back the noose, say Cumbrians'.

I was once sent to do a vox pop in another county. For years we'd run stories saying that Primark was looking to open in Carlisle. Surveys asking people what would most improve life in the city reported the same answer: Primark. I was ready to throw myself off something tall at the thought that this was the thing most desired by my fellow citizens.

In 2015 Primark finally confirmed that it was coming to Carlisle. I was dispatched with a photographer to Darlington, 80 miles away. That town has a similar demographic to Carlisle, and it already had a Primark. I was to ask the locals what they thought was so good about it.

During the journey I tried to work out what to say to them. 'Hello. I'm from a newspaper in Cumbria. We're so backward there that we want nothing more than a shop selling cheap clothes. Oh, and we've heard about this thing called electricity. What's it like?'

The job was less horrific than I'd feared. People humoured me and told me what they liked about Primark: mainly 'It's cheap.' The feature included a picture of me interviewing a young woman who'd just come out of the shop. I'm holding my notebook and pen while talking to her. She's looking at me with an expression which says, quite unequivocally, 'Who the *fuck* is this?'

12

Hard News

O N the morning of Wednesday 2 June, 2010, I interviewed Philip Day, the owner of Edinburgh Woollen Mill. He was Cumbria's wealthiest resident. Within a few years he'd be worth more than a billion pounds. We'd been trying to get an interview for a long time. I returned to the newsroom shortly after midday, expecting colleagues to ask me about him. Instead they were concerned with something else.

There'd been reports of shootings in west Cumbria. The police were telling people to stay indoors. The full story emerged in the coming days. Early that morning, fifty-two-year-old taxi driver Derrick Bird had left home with a shotgun and a rifle. He drove to his twin brother's house and shot him eleven times, killing him. He then drove to the home of the family's solicitor, killing him with two shots to the head.

At 10.30 Bird arrived at the Whitehaven taxi rank where he worked. He called over fellow driver Darren Rewcastle and shot him dead. In the next few minutes he shot three more taxi drivers, wounding them. Those victims were the last ones he knew. Bird then drove south along the coast road, firing at passers-by and calling people to his taxi before shooting them in the face.

Two hours after leaving Whitehaven, he drove to a wood and killed himself. By then Bird had shot dead twelve people and injured eleven others.

Early that afternoon, little of this was clear. Some of our reporters headed to west Cumbria. I asked to go but was told to write the Philip Day profile. It was the cover story for that Friday's *Cumberland News* features supplement and had to be finished next morning. If the extent of the tragedy had been apparent then, the plan might have been ripped up and I might have gone. Or maybe not. There was a clear distinction between news and features. A mass shooting was news, in every sense.

My colleagues did a superb job. Some of them arrived in west Cumbria before the police had announced that the killer was no longer a danger. I was frustrated to not be there myself. My chance came a few weeks later. I'd been desperate to climb aboard such a massive story and show what I could do with it.

Those thoughts faded when I saw the impact of a massive story on those for whom it's something bleaker than a career opportunity. In their small, dark living room, Darren Rewcastle's parents seemed broken. Darren's mother, Betty, discovered her son was dead while watching a TV newsflash. She saw a body on the ground at the taxi rank, covered by a blanket. 'I knew it was him by his feet. His new trainers. It was just him. Our Darren.' Even now, when she heard a car outside, she'd think it was Darren. Then she'd remember.

> I see the counsellor every week, and the doctor because I'm on tablets. I go to bed. I take my tablets. I have about two hours' sleep. Then I just see his body there. I see his feet sticking out. His trainers. That's all I see now. His body in the road. All day long . . . If I could have got there I would have gone over to be near him. To me, he was lying there all on his own.

Darren had moved back in with his parents after his marriage broke down. His bedroom was untouched since the morning he left it for the last time. Betty spent much of the interview sobbing. I wondered why she was putting herself through this, and concluded that she was determined to pay tribute to her son. Maybe talking helped her as well.

The interview involved little skill on my part. It was simply a case of being sympathetic, listening and writing. There was no mystery about what to ask. Her answers were ready to pour out. I felt nagging guilt at the knowledge that what she was saying was so grimly compelling. News has been described as what someone doesn't want you to know. Features can be what someone wishes with all their heart had never happened.

I also interviewed Paul Wilson, the third of the four taxi drivers shot by Bird. Bird stopped his cab when he saw Paul walking down the street and shouted, 'Oi, Paul!' Paul, who thought of Bird as a friend, approached his open window. Bird shot him in the face. Eleven shotgun pellets had lodged in Paul's right cheek. When I met him, that side of his face was lined with scars. Four pellets remained under the skin. Surgeons said removing them could damage nerves.

Darren Rewcastle's mother told me that if she saw a picture of Derrick Bird, she stabbed it with a pen. Paul had found forgiveness. 'Derrick was a nice guy. It wasn't in his character to do what he did. I've no ill feelings towards him. It's easy to dismiss him as a madman when you didn't know him. But when it's a member of your own community it's not so easy to say he's a weirdo and a psycho.'

The following year's inquest into the killings would hear that Bird was worried he'd be sent to prison for tax evasion, and felt he was victimised by some fellow drivers. Resentment and anxiety simmered and spilled over.

I wasn't sure whether to be impressed by Paul's forgiveness. Maybe it showed a lack of understanding towards the families of those who died. He'd seen a friend disintegrate and felt this wasn't the man he knew. But that was no consolation to Darren Rewcastle's mother. Perhaps Paul was high on life after coming so close to death. 'It wasn't my time, I suppose. I'm spared. I'm here. What's the point in wasting the time I've got by dwelling on it?'

Our papers were praised for their sensitive treatment of the tragedy. There was one major misstep. A week after the shootings, a minute's silence was held across Cumbria. Next day the *News & Star*'s front page featured the victims' photographs with the headline 'Always in our thoughts'. That would have been fine, except that the pictures included Derrick Bird's. His image was in the bottom-right corner. He looked as if he was smirking.

Angry readers rang to ask what we were thinking: classing Bird as a victim and putting his picture among those he murdered. No one in the newsroom admitted responsibility, as was usually the case with a monumental fuck-up.

The only one that came close was another *News & Star* front page years earlier. There'd been a male streaker at a rugby match involving a Cumbrian team. The front page was a picture of him with his genitals clearly visible. No blurring. No rugby ball overlaid to humorously hide his modesty. Just his dick on display. Many of the phone calls that day came from the newsagents who refused to sell the edition. The newsroom copies were quickly removed and the few of us who saw it were left wondering if we'd imagined the whole thing.

***

Torrential rain has always been an unwelcome feature of the Cumbrian climate. During my youth it never lasted longer than a few hours. In recent years it's gone on for days.

Three rivers run through Carlisle. In January 2005 much of the city, along with many other parts of Cumbria, flooded after exceptional rainfall. In Carlisle 1,600 homes were affected. Residents didn't return for months. Some couldn't face going back at all. In the following years flood defences were built. People thought it couldn't happen again.

Exceptional rainfall wasn't exceptional any more. After 2005 the defences saved Carlisle several times. Then came Storm Desmond. Its wind and rain battered much of the UK, nowhere more than Cumbria.

On the first Saturday night of December 2015 I walked down Warwick Road, Carlisle's main eastern thoroughfare. This densely populated area had suffered most in 2005. Now there were flood warnings for Carlisle after days of heavy rain. But Warwick Road seemed in denial. Through bay windows I saw people watching TV as Christmas lights twinkled. The Beehive pub looked packed. The only water on the road was drizzle. Maybe it would be OK.

Next morning, Warwick Road was a river. Cars were submerged. Brown water lapped the Victorian townhouses. From the water's edge I watched fire service and Coastguard crews bringing people to safety in dinghies. The scene was calmer and quieter than you might have expected. It felt like stunned silence, or respect for those within earshot whose lives were being wrecked again.

TV crews stood alongside me. Carlisle was again unwillingly in the national spotlight. A rescued woman returned to dry land and responded to an interview request with 'I just need a cup of tea.'

I'd been here, at Warwick Road's junction with Aglionby Street, eleven years earlier. This time the devastation was even worse. Storm Desmond deluged already saturated ground. It broke the UK's rainfall record. At Honister Pass in the Lake District, almost 14 inches fell in twenty-four hours. Across Cumbria three bridges were washed away and hundreds damaged. Nearly 7,000 homes and businesses were flooded: more than 2,000 of them in Carlisle.

The highest concentration of pain was again in the Warwick Road area. And that Sunday morning, the water was still rising. People whose homes were so far safe were desperate to protect them. I recognised a woman who was carrying sandbags. She was a B&B owner I'd once interviewed. I spent a few minutes helping her. It was a welcome chance to assist in a tangible way rather than telling myself that what I wrote about something might make a difference. Her business didn't flood. I knew that the next few weeks would be dominated by the stories of people who'd been less fortunate.

Next day I drove to a village near Carlisle and met a couple whose home had just flooded for the fourth time in eleven years. It was up for sale when Storm Desmond struck. 'Who'd buy this, complete with its own waterfall?' asked Susan, the woman of the house. She was remarkably good-humoured. Some neighbours arrived, one of whom had not been flooded. 'We're not speaking to her!' said Susan. Then she found a favourite book that had been destroyed. At that point, she left the room.

Her husband acknowledged that the amount of rain had been unprecedented and said that things would have been even worse without recently built flood defences. I wondered if I could have been so dignified.

The village pub, parish hall and school had flooded. All remained closed for months. The headteacher broke down at the end of our interview. 'It's the children, it's the time of year. They'd been practising so hard for Christmas plays. All I kept thinking about on Sunday night was the costumes floating about in the muck.'

Elsewhere I spoke to a woman who'd been rescued from her roof by a Coastguard helicopter, because the water was too treacherous for boats. 'It's unbelievable. You don't think that's ever going to happen. From putting the Christmas tree up in the afternoon to that.'

The water took a couple of days to leave the Warwick Road area. It was trapped inside the defences it had poured over. Warwick Road was the opposite of a golden mile. Pavements were piled with muddy Christmas trees and rubbish that used to be furniture and carpets.

I spoke to people who on Saturday night had known that Carlisle's rivers were rising, had moved prized possessions upstairs, hoped everything would be OK, and realised it wouldn't be. Those evacuated included heavily pregnant women, families with babies, the ill and infirm. Fire and Coastguard crews had travelled to Cumbria from across the north. There were also volunteers. A fourteen-year-old Sea Cadet rescued people in a canoe, floating halfway up the stairs of one house.

Some helped others while their own homes flooded. Community centres gave food and shelter. Neighbours offered meals and clothes. Donations to Cumbria's flood appeal poured in from around the country. We told the story of a community uniting in adversity, with one exception. On the morning of the floods, as thousands of people became homeless, one Carlisle estate agent trebled its 'admin charge' for new tenants to £600.

This was condemned in the national press: a city pulling together while one of its businesses tries to profit from misery. We ran what seemed to me to be a fairly half-hearted story. The company was a major advertiser with the *Cumberland News*, and if we'd given them a kicking we may have lost their custom. Instead I felt we risked losing readers' respect.

The disruption affected many aspects of life. A bridge that carries traffic to the north of Carlisle was closed for more than a week over concerns that it would collapse. A secondary school that had flooded for the second time moved elsewhere and never came back. McVitie's biscuit factory was shut for months. A nationwide shortage of ginger nuts and custard creams brought Carlisle back into the headlines.

The Beehive's staff and customers moved temporarily to the upstairs of a city-centre pub. I'd recently interviewed the Beehive's managers about their pub's refurbishment: it had been completed just weeks before Storm Desmond. They'd been in charge when the pub flooded in 2005. Now the landlord told me, 'It probably took us seven or eight years since the last flood to let go, to stop walking down to look at the river level when it's been raining heavily.' The landlady said, 'I don't think we'll ever feel comfortable again now.'

Fear of further flooding was something I heard a lot. Perhaps life was even harder for those who'd been here before. They knew they faced months of temporary accommodation, insurance companies, loss adjusters and builders. It wasn't a fun time for me or my colleagues either. I spent long days walking cold streets lined with overflowing skips; standing in living rooms with warped floorboards, listening to people trying to see a bright side and not always succeeding. I lived near Warwick Road. The country's biggest flood zone began a few hundred yards from my home. Within minutes I could leave the pain behind.

After Christmas the cavalry arrived in vans, not boats. Parts of

Carlisle were ghost towns, empty except for builders and a few people living upstairs or in caravans on driveways.

I visited an industrial estate whose businesses had flooded again. John Osborne, seventy-two, and Joe Earl, sixty-eight, had been repairing commercial vehicles here for thirty years. Storm Desmond wiped out any plans for retirement. They'd recently signed a long lease and were not optimistic about being able to sell it. 'I would like to retire,' said Joe. 'But who's going to buy it? There's nothing else but to carry on.'

I heard a lot of this very Cumbrian stoicism, and admired it. I also wondered whether making a fuss might have been more effective in securing better flood defences or some other measure to prevent a city being engulfed by water every few years.

The owner of a carpet shop was less philosophical about the defences failing to keep out unprecedented rainfall. He was Irish, which may explain his refreshing candour. 'When you put up a crash barrier, you don't build it to withstand a Fiat Panda hitting it. You build it for a lorry.'

It was a family business, run with his wife and two sons. He said it took them fourteen days to empty the contents of the shop into skips. 'Continuous emptying. Boxes and boxes of it. When we'd cleaned everything out it suddenly dawned on us: we've got nothing.'

Two months after Storm Desmond, one woman told me she'd cried all her tears. As she continued talking, that turned out to be untrue. 'There's people you've never even met before putting their arm round you, saying "Come on, let me give you a hand." It really touches you.'

That interview took place in the newly reopened Beehive. As I entered, the landlady yelled, 'Get him out of here!' I hoped she was joking but wasn't sure. I'd called in to the pub's temporary city-centre home several times, asking how things were, dredging up raw memories, asking ugly questions such as 'Do you worry it will happen again?'

Of course she did. Everyone did. Someone else told me, 'It's going to flood again. I know it is. We don't say "If it happens." It's "When it happens."' People stood on bridges after days of rain, gauging the height of the water and hoping.

A year on, dozens of houses were still empty. 'For Sale' signs jostled for attention. Many people sold cheaply just to get away. Others refurbished their homes and crossed their fingers.

Even two years after Storm Desmond, some homes were still unfit to live in, mainly due to shoddy work by sub-contractors. I interviewed a couple who were about to spend a third Christmas out of their house, having been given twenty dates for moving back in. The house had no internal doors. Wires dangled overhead from rows of beams. Slabs of plaster dropped from the kitchen walls with a tap. The husband said, 'It's very stressful – extremely. I'm waking up at three o'clock in the morning with things going through my head. The worst thing is, you can't do anything. You're powerless.'

Thousands of people knew the feeling. Storm Desmond cost Cumbria more than £500 million. The damage wasn't just financial. The memory and the threat of a repeat remained in the collective consciousness. It took nearly four years for work to begin on improving Carlisle's flood defences. The work quickly halted, because the ground was too wet.

***

Big stories are easy to write. Gathering information might be difficult. But the fact that it's an intriguing subject carries the writing along. The journalist knows that readers will be interested so the writing doesn't need adornment. Although the journalist's enthusiasm is likely to add some zest.

I didn't feel that way on 9/11. Within minutes of the second plane hitting the World Trade Center, two of my fellow feature writers had dashed into the centre of Edinburgh to find some American tourists. I didn't offer to join them. Weren't events in New York, Washington and Pennsylvania compelling enough? What would some Americans in Scotland saying that it was terrible really add? It wasn't our story. It was big enough to speak for itself with no need to localise it.

Maybe that argument is a way of justifying my inaction. Maybe I should have gone out. Six years later that feeling encouraged me to wade into the biggest story in Britain.

In August 2007 I was on holiday in Portugal. Since May that year the media back home had been obsessed with the disappearance of three-year-old Madeleine McCann from her room at a resort in Praia da Luz. A few days into my holiday, I discovered that Praia da Luz was about 20 miles away.

Next day I went there. It would have seemed like a dereliction of duty if I hadn't. But it was hard to switch from holiday mode to this, like being woken from a restful sleep to tackle an assault course. When asking people for an interview I was too embarrassed to say which paper I worked for, in case they asked a perfectly reasonable question like 'What's it got to do with you?'

There were posters of Madeleine in some, but by no means all, shop windows. Life seemed to have returned to normal, a state encouraged by business owners. One English shop worker I spoke to wanted the McCanns to go home. He felt their presence in the town made it no likelier that their daughter would be found, although he sympathised with them. 'Would I do the same in their situation? Of course I would. God knows how I would feel. But the truth is, life goes on.'

A waitress said she had a friend who used Second Life: the online virtual world in which people invent new identities for themselves. In cyberspace, her friend's alter ego was looking for Madeleine. 'It's weird . . . very weird,' she said.

In a supermarket, Madeleine's face stared out from the front pages of the English papers. That face had been watching us all summer. Madeleine had been everywhere and nowhere. She'd been looking at us as we were looking for her.

13

Website Woes

I N 2005 the *Cumberland News* was selling about 39,000 copies each week: close to its highest-ever sales figure. The *News & Star* was selling 26,000 a day: a slight fall since I'd started at CN Group a decade earlier. At this point the figures began a decline which, over the next few years, would plunge off a cliff.

At the end of the 1990s, CN had launched websites for each of its papers around Cumbria. These mainly featured news that people could have found elsewhere, such as road crashes, which would be reported by local TV and radio. The vast majority of our newspapers' content did not go online. If you wanted our product, you had to buy our papers. Why would we give our work away?

That was a question my colleagues and I continued to ask as more and more content was placed on our website. At first, stories would appear a day or so after print publication. Then they were published on the day the paper came out. Eventually some appeared on the website before they'd been in the paper. To most of us this seemed a suicidal policy: give away stories one day and expect people to pay for them the next. But it was pursued by local and national newspaper groups around the country.

We were told that newspapers and websites had different audiences. People who read our websites didn't buy our papers, so we were gaining extra readers. And people who bought our papers didn't look at our websites.

117

This might have been true at first. But it was no surprise that making the contents of newspapers available free to anyone with a computer or a mobile phone led to a collapse in newspaper sales. We'd created competition for our own papers. We damaged the part of the business that made lots of money by feeding a part that made much less.

The money we earned from selling papers slumped. Because sales declined, we also lost much of our papers' advertising revenue: their biggest source of income. Publishers thought that website advertising would cover the shortfall. It didn't come close. Many companies weren't keen to advertise on newspaper sites: to become one of the flashing, popping-up distractions that infuriate readers. And at CN as elsewhere, journalists' suggestions that papers should charge for access to their websites were dismissed as ignorant.

I felt that the rush to digital was fuelled by executives' fear of being seen as dinosaurs in a changing world. It wasn't based on evidence of revenue. We heard a lot about how many people were viewing our website, and very little about how much money this generated.

By the end of the 2010s, newspaper publishers that were more than a decade into their 'digital transformation' still made the vast majority of their money from print, even though print revenues had been decimated by giving their work away on their websites. Reach is the UK's biggest news publisher. Its papers include the *Daily Mirror*, *Daily Express* and *Manchester Evening News*. In 2019, the print part of the business provided 84 per cent of its income.

Much of the online advertising revenue that publishers had anticipated increasingly went to Facebook and Google instead: more about that later.

By the time it was clear that newspaper websites didn't pay their way, readers were used to reading local news for free online.

By fighting against piracy, the music and film industries maintained the view that their work should be paid for. The newspaper industry encouraged the idea that its product was worthless.

Around the newsroom there were plenty of analogies for CN Group's internet strategy. It was likened to a car manufacturer giving away its vehicles, then boasting that more people were now driving them. A colleague said, 'A baker wouldn't say "I had ninety-thousand people looking at my pies yesterday." He'd be more interested in how many he sold.'

When I was out and about, people told me, 'I used to buy the paper but I don't bother now because it's all on your website.' These people – newspaper readers who had stopped buying newspapers because their content was free online – did not exist, according to some newspaper bosses.

Publishers were caught in a perfect storm. Newspapers were hit by the recession that followed the 2008 financial crisis. And the internet hurt papers in ways their publishers couldn't control.

Newspapers' big advertising moneymakers had always been cars, homes, jobs and classified ads: people selling goods such as kitchen appliances, and tradespeople advertising their services. Now all these garages, estate agents, other companies and individuals didn't need newspapers. They could advertise on their own websites or on platforms such as Facebook and eBay.

Local papers also had countless online rivals providing information. Companies, public bodies and individuals could tell their stories without us. The BBC's website provided news free of charge. National newspaper sites followed suit. But we still had a great deal of exclusive content, which we chose to give away.

I should mention that not all journalists agree with my view that rushing to put stories online for free was a mistake. They see people like me as hopelessly behind the times. They probably think – correctly – that we turn up for work wearing animal pelts, our faces daubed with blood. I should also mention that many of those digital evangelists have the word 'digital' in their job title.

Perhaps living my formative years with newspapers rather than websites coloured my opinions. By the turn of the millennium, as the internet's influence rapidly grew, I was already twenty-nine. The feeling that your age influenced your view of the web was reinforced at an awards do in the early 2010s. An old-school colleague seemed reluctant to embrace the digital era. He made a speech in which he dismissed social media, referring to Twitter as 'Twatter'. That earned the night's biggest round of applause.

Since the 1800s CN Group and its predecessors had been locally owned by the Burgess family. By the 2000s, CN was one of Britain's last independent newspaper publishers. Most of them had been bought by the handful of companies that dominated the local newspaper market.

Robin Burgess, the fourth generation of his family involved in the business, became CN's chief executive in 1985. In the days when it made big profits he turned down lucrative offers to sell, partly due to the belief that communities were best served by locally owned papers.

CN was regarded as a good employer. There were nights out paid for by the company, Christmas lunches when managers were waiters, a staff newspaper, long-term sick pay for employees with serious illness or injury. When the annual report was published Robin would visit every CN office, across Cumbria and beyond, answering questions about the business. I didn't know of anyone who doubted his commitment to the company and its workforce. But it was easier to be benevolent when owning a local paper was a licence to print money.

The financial crisis and the slump in newspaper sales and advertising saw CN become more like a bigger company. In 2009 came the first of several waves of redundancies, most of them voluntary at that stage. The canteen was closed, as were most of our district offices. Pay was frozen.

In the next few years our papers' late editions were scrapped in an attempt to save money. The papers started being printed overnight rather than on the morning of publication, to extend their shelf life. Both these moves killed their ability to carry breaking news. Our delivery staff were laid off and the papers were distributed by a national company. The loss of our branded vans felt like a metaphor for us becoming less visible in our communities.

***

Before our website, we'd never really known what our readers thought of what we did, other than from their letters and phone calls. We conducted surveys in which they told us there was too much doom and gloom in our papers. We'd consider this before dismissing it. Because almost every big-selling edition had a splash about a fatal road crash or a murder.

There was no way to be certain about which stories were most read in our papers. But our website allowed us to see exactly how many views each story had online. This confirmed the feeling that bad news was good news for us. Crashes, violent crime and extreme weather usually topped the most-read chart. Pubs and shops opening or closing were also popular.

None of this was great for a feature writer. A one-paragraph weather warning could attract many more views than one of my carefully crafted profiles or colour pieces. As long as newspapers remained the company's priority, this wasn't a huge issue. There was an assumption that the people still buying papers wanted something in-depth. As the focus on our website grew, those of us writing about anything other than disasters and shops felt increasingly insecure.

By the time we launched a *Cumberland News/News & Star* Facebook page in 2011, the *Cumberland News*'s circulation had slumped to 26,000. It had lost a third of its sales in six years. The *News & Star* was selling 16,000 – a fall of almost 40 per cent.

One news editor, perhaps trying to deflect any blame from the quality of our stories, suggested that the weather played a part. It was either lashing down, so people didn't go out to buy a paper, or it was scorching, so they couldn't be bothered to buy a paper. We sniggered at this theory. But maybe CN Group really was a victim of climate change. If Cumbria wasn't under water it was baking in a heatwave or battered by gales. Conditions were conducive to buying a paper one morning in April and for half an hour in September.

Putting links to our website's stories on our Facebook page accelerated the decline in newspaper sales. Our Facebook policy was geared towards increasing 'engagement' with readers. As far as I could see, this consisted largely of them telling us that we were crap.

Posting a story on Facebook was throwing it to the wolves. Our choice of stories, our headlines, our pictures and our writing all came in for criticism from people who hadn't paid a penny to look at them. Popular comments included 'Slow news day?' and 'This is not news.' Some posted video clips of people shrugging their shoulders, with the caption 'Who gives a shit?' I'd thought readers would be grateful to have a free source of local news and opinion. Apparently not.

> The article tells us what time the programme was aired on thursday. Might have been useful to say what time it was repeated on sunday.

Please accept our apologies, madam. Would you like us to come round and give you a foot massage?

Some people commented on stories they obviously hadn't read, or asked a question that was answered in the first paragraph. Many Facebook users seemed perfectly pleasant. But we were at war with others. Or rather, they were at war with us. The hatred was extraordinary. Dozens of them devoted much of their time to attacking us.

A colleague wrote a column saying he was puzzled by the fuss over a royal baby. One Facebook comment said it was a pity his mother 'didn't swallow. She would of saved us from his irrelevant story.'

Someone else wrote, 'What a pointless, poorly written article for a supposedly professional paper.' That brought the response 'Professional paper', followed by two 'crying with laughter' emojis. Those scrunched-up faces, a tear squirting from each eye, made my right eye flicker in fury. They felt like a mocking attempt to shut down debate. A refuge for people who lacked any arguments to support their viewpoint.

Readers' opportunities to comment on our stories online coincided with our papers being worse than they used to be, after redundancies. But this lot would have crucified Shakespeare. Seeing our work greeted by a tide of poison was disheartening. I was annoyed that we were pandering to people who delighted in baiting us.

We posted a story to our Facebook page about the importance of local journalism, to highlight the News Media Association's Trusted News Day. The story included a picture of the editorial team. This was the chance some people had been waiting for.

Many of the following comments were marked 'Top contributor'. This was a Facebook label to reward those people who wasted a particularly large portion of their lives spouting opinions online.

'Top contributor' looked incongruous on our Facebook page when placed alongside such comments as:

> what a shit squad you have there.

> As if a picture of all the gossip demons are gonna make people believe the shit you print.

> Overpriced and local reporters hmm and yes you are terrible at typeset.

> Bollocks hairy sweaty ones the drivel you have churned out lately beggars believe.

> I'd rather trust Jimmy saville babysitting than what's printed by this lot.

> Well News and Star what do you say to all those comments. It seems every post is saying roughly the same thing. YOUR PAPER IS SHITE, YOU EMPLOY [emoji of a clown] THAT CANT MANAGE TO SPELL (I would of thought spelling was a fairly important skill in the newspaper industry).

> Ha loads of rubbish! Full of spelling mistakes and due to the internet making no money! I give it 5 years or less then bankrupt hopefully.

Our online readers often wished for our demise, and therefore for coverage of local councils, courts, etc. to end. Maybe these were people whose court cases we'd reported. Some of the comments that insulted us were never hidden from public view. It was like a shop having 'WANKERS!' daubed across its windows and not bothering to clean it off.

In fairness to our readers, they didn't hate just us. They had venom to spare for the people we wrote about. Politicians and criminals were among those routinely mocked and vilified, although some criminals were defended by family members:

> They took rap fore someone else so what u want them to be a snitch witch my family ain't think your a snitch go get a life please son.

Those readers who accused us of peddling – or pedalling – fake news may have got much of their news from dubious online sources. Some of our stories were indeed crap. But they weren't 'fake' or biased. The only agenda we had was getting a paper out every day and making it as good as possible.

The idea that we could afford to alienate half our potential readership by being biased towards left or right was ludicrous . . . usually. The exception was the rare occasions when political parties paid for a four-page wraparound of our papers, which included a version of the front page with a political message.

The decision to run these was commercial, not editorial. They were despised in the newsroom. But, hugely regrettable and damaging to our credibility as they were, they were labelled as adverts. And to show our neutrality, as well as our desperation for cash, we sold them to Labour and the Tories.

The response from my bosses when I complained about Facebook was along the lines of 'Yes, there are plenty of knuckle-draggers out there. But Facebook helps our website to get page views. And the more page views we get, the more businesses will pay to advertise on the site.' I thought businesses were more likely to run a mile than risk being associated with some of the comments on our website and Facebook page.

Those comments that had a particularly impressive number of swear words and libels were hidden by a news editor as soon as they were spotted; probably while their blood pressure soared and they wondered if that vacancy at the county council press office was still open.

Some of the gems on our Facebook page and website were in response to a colour piece I wrote about the abuse traffic wardens suffer every day. One warden recalled a recent incident when a young man got out of his car and said, 'I hope your wife dies of cancer.' The warden's wife had died of cancer.

I thought that even our Facebook readers would be sympathetic. Many were. Some just added to the abuse. Comments that were hidden included, 'Why the fuck would anyone wanna be 1 of them cunts anyways.' Someone who criticised this was advised to 'fuck off ya nonse'.

Another reader observed, 'Scum of the planet them lot u see em jus hanging about waiting to jus slap a ticket on ya car I can honestly say I am 1 of the lot that shouts wanker out me window as I gan past but I make sure to stick me head out so they know where it came from.'

One hidden comment was written on a story about a nightclub closing. The story was illustrated with a picture of the lane where the club was situated. This prompted one reader to stroll down memory lane. 'Fingered a few birds in that alley back in the day. Good times.'

A story about an open day at Carlisle's mosque prompted so many offensive comments that we removed it from Facebook. Facebook made a fortune from advertisers using it to reach people who read journalists' work there. But the company did little to deal with inflammatory reaction from its users. Newspapers' Facebook pages were a journalistic Wild West.

***

As fewer people read newspapers, fewer wrote letters. The angry ones I'd received in my early years had become a distant memory. Any letters at all were now, to use a favourite phrase of the old-school news editor, as rare as rocking-horse shit. It had reached the stage where I genuinely believed that if I'd received a letter calling me a wanker, I'd have punched the air in delight.

The ease of leaving a comment online left no doubt that my stories were still being read, for better or worse. My features escaped relatively unscathed. But not my weekly column. I used to think I was my own harshest critic. Readers' Facebook comments showed this definitely wasn't the case. I thought it was possible, and important, to write about serious issues in an irreverent style. This seemed to wind some people up.

How small-minded lytollis. Grow up!!

Roger......do you actually get paid for writing this rubbish.

Several readers asked that question. It made me feel small. Columnists are vulnerable. Even when we're not revealing anything about ourselves, it's all us. There are no interviewee's quotes to fall back on. It's just our idea of what's funny or interesting. If someone hates it, that's hard not to take personally.

My heart pounded when I prepared to look at my column online. One column had the headline 'Why we 40-somethings are too old to go clubbing'. It was obviously light-hearted, laughing at myself for being past it. Facebook comments included, 'What a load of crap! Who cares what some prat who doesn't like clubbing or dancing thinks about older people who go clubbing and dancing? Enjoy your sad, judgemental life, and let others enjoy their fun, however they choose to have it!!'

At times like that I wondered whether people had read the story and, if they had, why they would react so aggressively. That column also prompted the classic riposte, 'Knob'. Like the crying with laughter emoji, that's a difficult one to crawl away from with any dignity.

Readers praised my work as well. But the ego boost quickly melted. Criticism lingered and burned. Being abused by readers was widely regarded as a badge of honour for journalists. I wasn't thick-skinned enough to see it that way, at least not until a few days had passed.

We were supposed to welcome interaction. I just wanted people to say I was brilliant. I told myself that some readers were too dense to appreciate my work: that I was having my writing criticised by people who struggled to spell the word 'A'.

The most gratifying response was seeing another reader defend me. One of the 'Do you get paid for this?' comments prompted someone to tell them, 'What a complete cretin you are.' That was a beautiful sight. They then exchanged insults, including, 'Gan boil your head in a bucket of piss', before things got really nasty: they corrected each other's spelling and punctuation.

Social media makes cowards of us. There were times when I backed away from writing something surreal or whimsical for fear of it being torn apart. I tried not to feel at the mercy of strangers' opinions. But what if the critics were right? If they were, their feedback was never constructive enough to do anything with. Other than retire.

Newspaper readers were now mainly older people who preferred to stick with tradition. I pictured them reading their paper with tea and toast, appreciating good writing. In my mind, online readers were bad-tempered due to too much time spent staring at a screen;

skim-reading everything and absorbing nothing; expressing their frustration with life by insulting or mocking whatever didn't tally with their views. People have always enjoyed taking the mickey out of local papers, with their wrongly captioned pictures and their stories about sheds being broken into. The internet increased the hostility and the ease of spreading it.

This happened around the same time as journalists being disliked more than ever following the phone-hacking scandal. In 2011 the *News of the World* – the UK's biggest-selling newspaper – closed after it was revealed that the paper had hacked the phone of murdered schoolgirl Milly Dowler, as well as the phones of celebrities, politicians and members of the royal family.

My colleagues and I were angry about this for the same reasons as everyone else, with the added dimension that the behaviour of a few national journalists reflected badly on us.

My colleagues worked long, unsociable hours including a lot of unpaid overtime. They didn't break huge stories every day but they kept Cumbria informed about councils, court cases, inquests and much more.

Our stories were frequently followed up by national papers. Chief reporter Phil Coleman discovered that a psychiatrist from New Zealand had spent twenty-two years working in the NHS with no qualifications. She was subsequently jailed. Phil's story prompted the General Medical Council to introduce stricter checks on staff.

Our many campaigns included helping to save the breast cancer unit at a local hospital, and launching Cumbria's air ambulance. Admittedly, not every campaign was quite so successful. One to save closure-threatened rural bus services was quietly dropped when it appeared that no one gave a shit. In the newsroom, the campaign had been dubbed 'Save our empty buses'.

14

Chasing Glory

MAYBE my teachers didn't give me enough praise. Or maybe I was born shallow and needy. Either way, the idea of winning an award appealed to me far more than was healthy. I thought some of my writing was pretty good, while realising that I might be a tad biased. How great it would be if other people in the industry decided I was worthy of recognition.

Some colleagues didn't seem to care about awards. They seemed secure enough to not hang their self-esteem on whether they could win a Perspex trophy. Weirdos.

In 2000 I was shortlisted at the North West Media Awards in two categories: Feature Writer and Young Journalist. It wasn't a glamorous event, held on a Friday lunchtime in a function room at Wigan Athletic Football Club. But I'd been excited about it for weeks. I still felt like a pretender, having entered journalism by an unorthodox route. If I won an award, I'd really belong.

There were just three people on each shortlist: I was bound to win at least one category. I didn't. I still had to go onstage to collect my runner-up certificates. Young Journalist entrants were under thirty. I was twenty-nine years and ten months old. Walking back to my table, I heard the compère say, 'I thought this was supposed to be the *Young* Journalist category?' Everyone laughed. Except me.

Since being shortlisted, I'd tried to prepare for not winning. I imagined the other names in my categories being read out. They would win – I wouldn't. When their names were indeed read out, I knew I'd been kidding myself. I'd really thought I would win. How could their work possibly be better than mine? I'd never read their work, but still.

In the next sixteen years I was shortlisted a further nine times in the Feature Writer category. I didn't win any of them. My colleagues' amusement grew with my bitterness. Eventually I don't think there was anyone in the newsroom who had never suggested that Beck's song 'Loser' should be played when I collected my certificate.

At one stage I was shortlisted six times in seven years. By then the ceremony had been switched to a Thursday night in November, normally in Chester, Liverpool or Manchester. It was a long round trip from Carlisle to watch someone else win, especially when it felt as if the judges were engaged in an epic wind-up.

The longer it went on, the more people told me, 'This has got to be your year.' I still attempted to convince myself that I wouldn't win. My reaction always told me that deep down I'd thought I would. I tried to look pleased for the winner. As the years went by, this became like twisting a corpse's face into a smile.

It didn't help that one of my best friends was the most prolific award winner in British journalism. Carlisle United reporter Jon Colman won at least one sportswriting award every year, and often several, deservedly so. One year I travelled back with Jon sitting on my left and Phil Coleman on my right. Both were clutching trophies. It was my tenth time returning home empty-handed.

On a different occasion my category's result had been among the first to be announced. I didn't win, obviously, and spent the rest of the evening drowning my sorrows before boarding the minibus home from Liverpool with about a dozen other CN Group employees.

We'd been on the M6 for an hour or so when the urge for a pee became desperate. There was no toilet on board. I was sitting on the back row. I started walking down the bus to ask the driver if we could stop at the next service station. I'd barely stood up when we passed the next service station.

We wouldn't reach another one for nearly an hour. I sat down, panic-stricken and in pain. My bladder felt on the verge of bursting. The future immediately became clear. I wouldn't be known as the journalist who failed to win lots of awards, or who maybe wasn't bad at his job. From now on it would always be: 'Lytollis . . . is he the one who pissed himself on the bus?'

Suddenly inspiration struck. It's impossible to urinate with an erection. All I had to do was bring myself to attention and the problem would be solved.

A colleague whom I knew well was the only other person on the back row, and he was asleep. There was nobody on the row in front and there were no lights on. Perfect. I put my right hand in my trouser pocket and tried to jiggle some life down below. No response. The jiggling became more frantic. Still nothing.

I felt my colleague rousing, which was more than I'd managed. 'What are you doing?' he said. I explained my predicament. He thought for a moment, said, 'Fair enough,' and went back to sleep.

I made it to the service station, in agony. By then I'd modified my technique to simply squeezing the end. At least that night I hadn't returned empty-handed.

I'm sharing this delightful tale because it feels like a metaphor for the hollowness of chasing glory. Your evening begins with champagne, cocktail dresses for the ladies, lounge suits for the men. And it ends with a furtive wank on a minibus.

***

In 2007 I'd been shortlisted in the Weekly Feature Writer category at the Regional Press Awards. Every local paper in the UK was eligible for these awards. The ceremony was in London. My excitement turned to dismay when I took my seat and looked in the programme. My photograph was one I'd never seen before. My expression was a blend of smirk and pout. My thumb and forefinger rested on my chin in a parody of the classic reporter's byline picture.

Then it clicked: this had been taken in the newsroom several years earlier. We'd all been snapped for an internal security system. The photographer had said these pictures would never be seen outside the building. But someone had sent mine to the awards' organisers.

It was taken soon after my Jordan embarrassment. Jordan had been pouting in that photo. I saw then that a pout is a way to control your expression. Narrow your eyes, push your lips out, hide your fear. I decided that whenever I felt nervous while being photographed, I'd pout. Here was the terrible result.

The picture was so bad, it left me wishing they'd used my passport photo. Years later I finally found the courage to show it to my girlfriend, having persuaded myself that maybe it wasn't as absurd as I'd thought. She immediately christened it 'Twat Face'. When my category was announced, that picture appeared on the screen. People laughed. I didn't win.

The winner was a colleague, which made it worse. I pretended to be pleased for them and nearly choked on my congratulations. I drank far too much and somehow made it to the hotel I'd booked. Once there, I spent several minutes spelling my surname to the receptionist. This is ridiculous – where do they find these people?

I'd gone to the wrong hotel. I spent most of the next morning throwing up.

A reporter was sick in her handbag on the bus back from another awards do, and was widely admired for it. My best friend at work vomited over himself on the train back from a ceremony. He reckoned his colleagues' reaction to this example of old-school journalism was easily the most acclaim he received in a twenty-year career.

The following year I was shortlisted at the Regional Press Awards again, and won. It felt as good as I'd hoped: the validation I'd been craving since I started in journalism thirteen years earlier. Colleagues and readers seemed pleased for me. But I learned that the etiquette following an award win is tricky. My natural response would be to say, 'I've won an award!' and get T-shirts printed. This would arguably be immodest.

Instead I had to keep shtum and hope that people found out without my help. If they said, 'Congratulations!' I'd adopt a puzzled expression and pretend to have no idea what they were talking about.

'Sorry?'

'Congratulations on your award!'

'Oh, right! Yeah – thanks very much.'

My award – I'd forgotten all about it. That thing I've had on my bedside table since the day I won it.

I won that category three years running, then it was scrapped. I assume there weren't enough feature writers left on weekly papers to make it viable. The *Cumberland News* was still one of the best weeklies in the country but many others were poorly resourced. There was now just one feature-writer category, for weeklies and dailies. I kept entering but was never shortlisted again now that I was competing with writers from big-city daily papers.

Maybe that was a blessing in disguise. These are miserable

affairs if you don't win. An awards host once told me that they're difficult events from his point of view. 'Everyone turns up in a good mood. But by the end, eighty per cent of them are losers.'

If I didn't win, the judges were clueless. If I did, thank God they'd finally found some who knew what they were doing. Journalists who fell by the wayside at any stage of the process could count on a sympathetic response from colleagues. In the days before awards entries were sent digitally, one reporter's envelope was returned to the newsroom. Her boss realised what it was, and used a stencil to write 'REJECTED' across it. The reporter was devastated. 'Why would the judges do that?' she asked. Nobody dared to tell her the truth.

After one North West Media Awards, I heard a TV reporter complain to an organiser that she'd been shortlisted three times without winning. Amateur. I didn't complain until my ninth defeat. And even then it was a jokey email, albeit with an anguished undercurrent.

In 2016 I was shortlisted for the eleventh time. That year the awards expanded to include publications from Staffordshire, Shropshire and north Wales. As if winning this thing wasn't proving hard enough. I spent the next few weeks moaning to everyone I met that Staffordshire and Shropshire are in the Midlands while north Wales is in . . . Wales.

As always, I told myself that I wouldn't win. Richard Ault would win. He was from the *Sentinel*, based in Stoke-on-Trent, Staffordshire. I'd been shortlisted ten times without winning. This fucker would turn up for the first time – from a paper that isn't even in the north-west – and win. And we shared the same initial. So for a split second I'd think they were announcing my name only to realise it was his.

Really, though, I thought I would win. There were only three people on the shortlist. I'd entered some strong features. And surely they wouldn't let me lose again. This was my year. My colleagues at the CN Group table all told me so. Here goes . . .

'And the winner is . . . Richard Ault – the *Sentinel*.'

The rest of the night passed slowly. One phrase played on a loop in my head. *Eleven times. Eleven fucking times.*

Maybe they could have given me an award to recognise the number of times I'd failed to win an award? I'd happily have been pitied or patronised if it got me a trophy and 'Simply the Best' playing as I strutted to the stage.

I knew that being shortlisted so often was an achievement. But I couldn't really put 'Didn't win at the North West Media Awards eleven times' on my CV. Somebody once said about Buzz Aldrin, 'He resents not being the first man on the moon more than he appreciates being the second.' I could identify with that. Not that I'm saying being a runner-up at the North West Media Awards is comparable with being the second man on the moon. That's for history to decide.

15

The Man with the Pigeon Tattoo

NEIL Hodgkinson left after nearly six years as editor and was replaced in 2012 by Dave Helliwell. The theory that each editor was very different from their predecessor again proved accurate. Dave was much quieter than Neil, a calming presence in a turbulent time.

I liked Dave. I think he liked me. But during my vox-pop years he obviously thought I wasn't suffering enough already. He decided that the *News & Star* should contain more about everyday life in our communities. That sounded like a great idea, until he decreed that feature writers should do it.

Grassroots journalism was traditionally the preserve of young reporters. They learned their trade by interviewing parish councillors and shopkeepers about potholes and window displays. Nothing too controversial, not too much scope for being sued. In the process they built contacts, honed their shorthand and interviewing skills, and gained a heightened news sense. Or not. Some of them weren't very good and stayed that way. But the principle was sound.

I was at the lofty peak of local journalism, writing profiles, colour pieces and columns. I'd worked at a big-city paper, for five whole months. I'd nearly won lots of awards. Why should I be tasked with community reporting? I was above all this. And it dawned on me, a little sadly, that I didn't have much interest in communities. I lived in a block of flats, largely because I didn't want to be part of a community. I wanted to come home, lock the door and not speak to anyone until the next day.

I had the sense not to use any of this as an argument against doing it. No need: I'd thought of other arguments. I asked for a meeting with Dave, and said I was concerned that the plan to have four pieces on each of these centre spreads meant there'd be no room for anything substantial. He said that wasn't the case, even though the longest story would be a measly five hundred words. Five hundred words is a feature writer's equivalent of a '*CU soon x*' text message.

I tried another tactic: would the idea work in our large circulation area? Would someone in Egremont want to read two pages of community news about Annan? Those towns are 60 miles and 90 minutes apart, the former in England and the latter in Scotland. Some news is big enough to interest anyone. But would the refurbishment of a community centre and suchlike have any appeal elsewhere? Dave thought so. And even if this content didn't travel well, readers could be confident that we'd be reporting from their town soon.

Oh well. I'd played all my cards so I'd just have to get on with it. The feature was given the title 'What's the Crack?' It was not about hard drugs, although there were times when these might have made the process easier. 'Crack' is the Cumbrian version of the Irish *craic*: a dialect word for news.

'What's the Crack?' would run from Monday to Thursday. There were four feature writers. We'd each do one a week. That didn't seem too bad. Then one of the four left, the week before it started. She hadn't seemed ecstatic about the job in general and 'What's the Crack?' was the final straw.

I had no doubt that there were amazing stories to be discovered.

But there wasn't time to knock on doors and find them. Instead we focused on pubs, shops and community centres: 'low-hanging fruit' as a colleague put it.

For my first 'What's the Crack?' I visited Longtown, eight miles north of Carlisle. I interviewed the father and son who'd run the local hardware shop for decades; a pub landlord; the owner of a new café; a councillor talking about the town's strengths and challenges. I even squeezed in the news that TV antiques expert Paul Hayes was coming to Longtown Community Centre. 'But the star of *Bargain Hunt* and *Cash in the Attic* will not be searching for forgotten treasures. He'll be playing classic rock 'n' roll with his band, The Paul Hayes Collection.'

To my surprise, I quite enjoyed it. My enthusiasm evaporated when it was published and I saw my byline picture. It was 'Twat Face'. The photo that was supposedly taken only for a security pass had been placed in the editorial system. A sub-editor, perhaps weary of my complaints about subs' work, had decided to use it.

I shuffled over to the chief sub. 'Please don't use that picture. I was told it would never be published. We've got lots of other pictures. Can you use one of those?'

'Yeah – no problem.'

'Twat Face' remained as my byline picture for 'What's the Crack?'s four-year run.

Initially I was obsessed with the idea that I should be high-lighting the community aspect of each place I featured. This manifested itself in asking everyone I interviewed, 'Is there a good sense of community around here?', to which they'd reply 'Yes.' I sensed that asking open-ended questions would lead to more interesting answers.

'What's the sense of community like around here?'

'Good.'

I visited towns and villages across north Cumbria for these features. Mainly I focused on Carlisle's estates, discovering parts of the city that I hardly knew. As a snapshot of society in the 2010s, 'What's the Crack?' was revealing. The sense of community that I kept being told existed seemed to be diminishing, even in a close-knit place like Cumbria.

Pubs and shops were closing. Charities and clubs were struggling to attract volunteers and members. It brought home how much was dying. I had the impression of a world in which people were exhausted by their jobs, and their leisure time was spent at home with TVs and computers. Or was that just me?

Writing four pieces for one spread was time-consuming, especially as I often had to do two 'Cracks' a week, along with numerous other features. The low-hanging fruit was quickly exhausted. I kept coming back and found it increasingly rotten.

Pub landlords and community centre managers must have been bemused by my frequent calls. I'd written about plans for a new kitchen at a Carlisle community centre. The progress of this minor story became an obsession. Every three months or so I'd write about that estate again and ring the centre's manager to ask if there was any more news about the kitchen. If there wasn't – and there usually wasn't – I'd rehash the original story with a new quote saying that progress was expected soon. When the kitchen finally opened, I gave it the kind of treatment normally reserved for royal weddings.

Amid the rotting fruit was an occasional ripe peach. Interviewing a man who kept pigeons, I noticed tattoos on his arms. When I asked about them, he rolled up his sleeves. Both arms were covered in portraits of birds he'd owned over the years. There in blue ink were Leona, Blanche, Phil's Choice and many more.

When someone had a great story, and they didn't know it was

a great story, I resisted the urge to say, 'Shit – that's amazing!' An overly enthusiastic reaction might make them feel self-conscious and prompt them to clam up. Instead it was a case of saying, 'Hmmm, those tattoos are rather nice,' then rushing back to the newsroom to put in a picture request. 'And make sure you get his arms – they're covered in tattoos of pigeons!'

The bird man told me, 'It's very emotional when they die. These are my friends. Not that long ago one of my favourite pigeons was slowly dying of old age. I wanted him to die in this place where he'd flown to all them times. He died in that corner nest box.'

When 'What's the Crack?' was placed in its corner nest box for the final time, I calculated that I'd done about three hundred of them. I wish that I'd found fewer community centre kitchens and more pigeon tattoos.

***

Although they could be painful to write, I saw the value for readers in vox pops and 'What's the Crack?' But some features were painful to write and to read. Every week the *Cumberland News* ran a page called 'Agenda'. This saw a topical issue being dissected to the tune of about 1,400 words. Some weeks, a body being dissected would have had more appeal.

There wasn't always an issue that merited such in-depth analysis. The space still had to be filled. We'd either choose something that didn't deserve the attention or we'd go back yet again to Brexit, or the struggle of shops to compete with online retailers, or the structure of local government in Cumbria.

Another bullet for feature writers to dodge was a weekly *News & Star* piece called 'Talking Point'. This saw four people being interviewed about a newsworthy topic. 'Agenda' took priority. So when it came to finding a 'Talking Point' subject, we were really scraping the barrel. I was hopeless at coming up with ideas for either.

'Any suggestions, Rog?'

'Yes: I've been thinking it's far too long since we wrote about Brexit.'

These features had been in our papers for as long as anyone could remember, and remained largely because no one could be bothered to think of something else. Our leader columns had also outstayed their welcome. Most papers ran leaders, normally on their letters page. They were the voice of the paper: its opinion on a major story. This may have been appropriate when people were more willing to be told what to think by their newspaper. By the time I started at CN Group they were already outdated. Our opinion carried as much authority as a drunk uncle's at a wedding.

Colleagues mocked other regional papers whose leader columns had referenced some minor local matter and demanded that the Prime Minister should intervene. In their defence, it did feel as if you were writing with a quill pen when tasked with a leader. A colleague told me he'd written about the need for transparency with an impending local council decision. He said, 'I found myself writing "It is not a matter for smoke-filled rooms." As soon as I'd finished the sentence, I looked at it and thought, "You pompous arsehole."'

During Keith Sutton's reign, the *Cumberland News* leader had been one of the most agonised-over parts of the paper. Various drafts would go back and forth between the editor and the writer. The writer was often me. This was supposed to be a source of pride; a sign that I was trusted with something important. But the feeling that it was a waste of time wouldn't go away.

In theory, the leader was a statement of the paper's position. In practice, we didn't dare alienate swathes of our readership by offering a different view to theirs. So we stated an opinion only when it was difficult for anyone to disagree with it. Someone has just been convicted of murder: murder is a bad thing. This is a bank holiday weekend: let's hope the weather stays fine to help the county's tourism industry.

The problem came when tackling a contentious issue, or one with no obvious solution. At this point, leader-writing became fence-sitting. I should have had the phrase 'A delicate balancing act' as a shortcut on my keyboard. Protecting the environment and the economy? The desire to fund an expensive but lifesaving drug? A delicate balancing act.

I wrote a leader about the finances of the trust that ran two local hospitals. 'How they can operate with nearly £250 million of debt hanging over them is a question with no easy answer.' 'No easy answer': textbook stuff.

I was convinced that hardly anyone read leaders. Occasionally I'd write one in the *News & Star* about a story that was then pulled from the paper. Due to the kind of cock-up that makes the newspaper industry such a stimulating place, the leader sometimes remained. I never heard of anyone asking why we'd published three hundred words about a non-existent story.

I had the privilege of being around at the birth of a part of our papers that was instantly obscure. One sub-editor liked chips. He used to write reviews of fish-and-chip shops: on the sports pages. It might seem as if I typed that while guzzling LSD. I can only swear – on Piers Morgan's life – that it's true.

The chief sub wasn't keen for one of his staff to be reviewing fish-and-chip shops when they could have been doing more important things, like ruining my features. The sub wrote them anyway, smuggling them on to a sports page at the last minute to minimise the chance of them being spotted and removed. This led to some of journalism's great juxtapositions. Reports of hard-fought wins for Workington Town sat alongside news that the cod at Joe's Plaice was melt-in-the-mouth delicious and the chips were crispy without being overdone.

Most of us read these with deep joy. They were weird and utterly ridiculous, thereby meeting two of the most important criteria in any newsroom.

16

Takeover

ROBIN Burgess retired as CN Group's chief executive in January 2016, although the Burgess family kept its majority share-holding. The declines in newspaper sales and advertising revenue had accelerated. A large chunk of our much-reduced profits was swallowed by the company's pension-fund deficit.

Robin's successor, an exuberant Scot called Miller Hogg, had a brief to cut costs further. Many reporters who left weren't replaced. Senior managers were laid off. CN always had a top-heavy man-agement structure. I had no idea what most managers did, even some of those in editorial.

One senior member of the editorial staff seemed untroubled by a strong work ethic. So he caused a stir one day by leaping from his seat and striding to the stationery cupboard. Grabbing a Bic pen, he hurried back to his desk. This was a turn-up. For the first time in years, he must have uncovered a story. He sat down, took the top off the pen, and began poking his ear with it.

Another colleague wrote a novel at work. Presumably they didn't know it was visible in the computer system we all used. There were regular informal conferences in which some of us discussed the plot, the characters, and what this person was being paid a great deal of money to do.

For all I knew, managers in other departments did amazing things for their salaries. But it didn't look that way as their presence failed to slow the decline. The same could have been said for me. At least there was no doubt about what I did, and I wasn't earning megabucks for it.

The company had begun increasing the price of its papers every nine months. Charging more for inferior products proved a dubious way to raise revenue. Like most papers, the *News & Star* was losing over 10 per cent of its sales each year. It was among the front runners in a very competitive category: worst-performing local daily paper in the UK. By 2016 it was selling just over 9,000 copies a day: a drop of more than 40 per cent in five years. This was a horrible situation. At the same time, I felt a morbid curiosity. How low could we go?

Most publishers were caught in the same vicious circle. Falling revenue led to cost cuts, which led to worse papers, which led to falling revenue.

At one staff briefing we were told we'd reached the stage where price rises didn't work any more. They lost us so many sales, they actually cost us money. But a few months later, to a soundtrack of head scratching, the prices went up again.

Against this background, in June 2016 it was surprising to see the company launch a new paper. *24*, subtitled *The North's National*, was a tabloid published from Monday to Friday and priced at 40p.

The theory was that the north of England was poorly served by London-based national papers. Here was an alternative, which would offer mainly northern stories. It was a narrow definition of the north. The circulation area was Cumbria, south-west Scotland, and slivers of Lancashire and Northumberland. Most of this patch was already covered by CN Group's papers so *24* could be added to existing deliveries.

I was asked to write a weekly column. *24*'s columnists were the only content not supplied by the Press Association news agency. This made it similar to *Metro*: the free paper available in cities including Manchester, Liverpool and Newcastle. *Metro*'s presence is one reason why *24* wasn't sold in those cities. But many of its stories were about them: stories that had little relevance in *24*'s corner of the north.

The paper lasted just six weeks. By the time the plug was pulled, it was selling fewer than 1,000 copies a day. Most of us wondered what the point had been of launching something that always seemed doomed to failure. Its publicity campaign was apologetic. The only places it was advertised were our other papers and the handful of local radio stations that CN owned at the time.

I bought *24* once on a day off, after hunting for it at my local newsagent whose owner had never heard of it. One of the free-lance subs who worked on *24* once tried to buy a copy in Carlisle at 3 p.m. The vendor tried to dissuade him. They hadn't sold any all day and didn't want to open the still-tied bundle for the sake of selling just one.

This episode did nothing for morale. More redundancies followed. The advertisement design team was laid off, with their work outsourced to Wolverhampton. One day we were gathered in the newsroom and told that Dave Helliwell had been made redundant after five years. He'd gone to a meeting that morning and been asked to leave the building immediately.

Dave had stood firm on the need to have a well-staffed news-room – a standpoint that never used to be regarded as controversial for a newspaper editor. But in this changing world that attitude may not have helped him. His departure was the kind of thing we'd heard about at bigger, more ruthless companies. Our picture editor suffered the same fate soon after. He was popular and hard-working, which counted for nothing.

After *24*, the next attempt to create revenue was an appeal to readers to give us money for using our websites. This was a first for the regional press. The *Guardian* had started doing it a few months earlier, with some success. But their writers were read by millions around the world: largely the kind of liberal audience that recognised the importance of journalism and was prepared to pay to help sustain it.

Did any of this apply to CN Group and its online readers? We were pretty sure of the answer. Around Cumbria our papers' editors were dragged in front of video cameras with varying degrees of enthusiasm, from very little to none at all, to talk about the importance of local news and the need to fund it. These videos were posted on our websites.

Group editor James Higgins issued a statement saying, 'We cannot continue indefinitely to offer our digital content for free. There has to be a return somewhere down the line for the investment we make in our local teams.'

Those of us who had long argued that online journalism didn't pay its way felt vindicated. But it was a hollow victory, considering that the company's strategy for covering the shortfall was to pass around a begging bowl. The appeal ran alongside a 'No to fake news!' logo. This felt rather cynical. I thought it was prompted less by concerns about fake news and more by our failing business model.

Readers were invited to make a donation, from £5 to £1,000. Finding out how much was given proved beyond the investigative skills of our reporters, and certainly me. It wasn't enough to prevent the appeal quietly disappearing after a few weeks and never being mentioned again.

Asking our readers to pay for something we were giving away seemed a desperate idea. Like the rest of the industry, CN was flailing around in search of solutions. In briefings Miller Hogg argued that it was better to try something and fail than to try nothing. I agreed in principle, although it depends what you're trying. Some ideas just led to loss of confidence in management.

It was easy to criticise. The only idea I had was to encourage more people to buy our papers, by making them better and by putting fewer stories on our website. By this stage it may have been too late. Readers had experienced too many years of free online news to readily return to papers.

And while many had Sky, Netflix and Amazon Prime subscriptions, the thought of spending money on a local news website horrified them. If our appeal had generated a pound for every online comment about us being reduced to begging, for every reader saying they looked forward to us going out of business, and for every crying with laughter emoji, we'd all have been driving gold-plated Ferraris.

CN Group management's questionable decisions just kept coming. Two weeks after our 'No to fake news!' logo first appeared, the *News & Star* sold its front page to the Conservative Party. The edition three days before the 2017 general election came in a wraparound. The front page featured a picture of Prime Minister Theresa May and the headline 'On Thursday: Vote to get Brexit Right'.

The damage to our credibility was enormous. I marvelled at the short-sightedness of grasping at cash with no thought to how that could be used against us. It inspired a new Twitter account called 'Not the News and Star'. Its anonymous creator wrote that they set it up to highlight the paper's right-wing bias. For proof, they argued, look no further than that Theresa May front page. There'd previously been a Labour Party wraparound before a county council election, which the account never mentioned.

This was the beginning of a long campaign. 'Not the News and

Star' delighted in highlighting our spelling and grammatical mistakes, as well as our supposed Tory leanings. Any interview with a Conservative MP or councillor was hailed as evidence. The account was guilty of the lack of balance it accused us of. All the times we wrote about Labour politicians and trade unions were ignored.

'Not the News and Star' also revelled in shouting about our plummeting sales figures when they were released twice a year. Newsroom conversation was dominated by theories about who was behind it. They seemed to know a lot about the newspaper industry, which made their sniping all the more irritating. They knew that many experienced staff had left, and the pressure this put on those who remained. But they consistently put the boot in.

We thought it must be an ex-employee. Maybe someone who'd been made redundant in one of the recent purges. Someone very bitter . . . the list of suspects was long.

One morning in February 2018, that mystery was overshadowed. We were asked to gather in the now defunct canteen for an announcement by Miller Hogg. He told us that CN Group was about to be bought by Newsquest, the UK's second-biggest publisher of local papers. We looked at each other in silence. I saw one woman crying. The days of CN being a cosy company had long gone. But no one expected Newsquest to be more benevolent.

Owned by US corporation Gannett, it was known for making massive profits – often tens of millions of pounds a year – while ruthlessly cutting costs. Some of my former colleagues had moved to papers that had been bought by Newsquest. Straight after the announcement I emailed one of them and asked, 'What can we look forward to?' They replied, 'Slashing, burning, that kinda thing.'

A few days later, some of Newsquest's top brass visited. Chief executive officer Henry Faure Walker did most of the talking. He spoke of his excitement at buying CN Group, which would soon become Newsquest Cumbria. Someone asked if there would be redundancies. He said it was likely.

Robin Burgess was not in good health by now. But the following month, during his last week of ownership, he visited all CN's offices to thank us for our efforts, and to say goodbye.

***

A week after the takeover, Newsquest announced plans to close our printing press with the loss of more than thirty jobs. Printing of all our papers transferred to Glasgow. Most staff in departments such as classified advertising and IT were laid off, with their work being done at Newsquest centres elsewhere. We used to run stories criticising companies for moving jobs out of Cumbria. I don't think we ever did that again.

Editorial was hit. Three of the four remaining photographers in Carlisle were made redundant, as were all but one of the photographers in our west Cumbria office, which also produced two weekly papers. We were left with two photographers to cover more than 1,000 square miles. A few months later the west Cumbria photographer was made redundant. Most of the remaining sub-editors were also laid off. Soon, just one remained in Carlisle.

Group editor James Higgins was among the first casualties. Chris Story became editor of the *Cumberland News* and the *News & Star*. Chris had started as a reporter and had been de facto editor for the previous year. He was relatively young for the job, in his late thirties, and retained an enthusiasm that would be tested by a frightening workload.

The role of editor had become very different. Keith, Neil and Dave used to spend most days in their office, coming into the newsroom mainly on Thursdays to check the *Cumberland News*. I presumed that the rest of the time they were in meetings to talk about budgets, strategies and whatever else editors discussed.

Chris did the meetings aspect of the job while also writing and subbing much of our papers. Based in the newsroom, he fielded countless enquiries from readers and colleagues. Staff shortages occasionally saw him cover reporting jobs: interviewing and taking pictures. His commitment was evident every day, working long hours while telling the rest of us to leave on time. The editor's job had been the most prestigious and sought after in the company. Now, few would have relished its constant firefighting as Newsquest threw petrol on the newsroom.

The departures continued. In editorial we'd see people summoned to a meeting room. Sometimes there'd be a fatalistic 'Here we go, then.' They'd return a few minutes later, often in tears. They'd been told their job was at risk and their future was subject to a 'consultation process'. I wasn't sure what to say to them. It was as if they'd been diagnosed with something nasty. A serious case of redundancy.

This happened throughout the building. A steady flow of emails announced that staff members from other departments were leaving. Many had been there for decades. Some were happy to get out. Some worried about the future. How much freelance work could there be for so many photographers? And sub-editing didn't seem like a transferable skill. 'What will you do when this goes tits up?' became a frequently asked question. I had no idea, and tried not to think about it. Being a journalist was not what I did, but who I was.

December brought another cull. The National Union of Journalists (NUJ) calculated that during its first nine months in Cumbria, Newsquest had made more than a hundred people redundant. Leaving do's happened most Friday nights. We reminisced about the good old days of more staff, more fun, more papers sold, and indulged in gallows humour about the state of the industry.

One sub brought several copies of his leaving page to the pub. Leaving pages were written and designed by colleagues in the style of the *Cumberland News* or the *News & Star*: the more insulting the better. They had to be produced in the editorial system. Everyone involved was terrified that the revelation of a reporter leaving because they'd been jailed for bestiality would end up as the splash in next day's paper.

At the end of the night I was horrified to see punters reading the departing sub's alternative *Cumberland News* front page – which accused him of professional incompetence and personal criminality – and perhaps wondering why the paper wasn't always this interesting.

I felt embarrassed when outsiders glimpsed the reality behind newspapers' holier-than-thou façades. See also: hoping visitors to the newsroom don't notice the mug shots of drug-addled criminals pinned to the walls for our amusement. Likewise, the legendary birdwatching report that had one sentence marked with fluorescent pen: 'The highlight of the weekend was a surprise shag on the cliffs at St Bees.'

Reporters and feature writers escaped the initial cuts. But we were now doing subs' jobs as well as our own. Newsquest's editorial system used templated pages. Sometimes I could choose the template. For a feature, they ranged from seven hundred words to seventeen hundred. If I was writing a news story, the shapes were chosen by news editors. (They were now known as audience and content editors. There was a very good reason for this. 'Audience and content editor' could be shortened to ACE, in an attempt to persuade people whose job involved sitting at a desk all day that they were actually fighter pilots or astronauts.)

In olden days we used to write each story knowing roughly

how long it had to be. Subs then made it fit. Now we had to make it fit by writing exactly enough to fill the shape. Some of these shapes appeared to be Newsquest's version of 'enough to paper the shithouse wall'. I'd write a news story, regard it as finished, and realise that the shape was bigger than the story merited. I needed to grind out perhaps another two hundred words to fill it.

Suddenly many of our stories ended with several paragraphs listing the shoe sizes, allergies and favourite breakfast cereals of everyone mentioned. This despite the fact that some of the stories were worth – as the sadly now retired old-school news editor would have put it – half of fuck all.

We also had to write the headlines, the picture captions and the kickers. Kickers, I learned, are the first part of a caption: normally one or two words followed by a colon. These could be frustratingly time-consuming. When writing about a charity walk I once spent five minutes agonising over a kicker, before typing 'Walk'.

Generally, though, that aspect of subbing wasn't too difficult. Whether my headlines, captions and kickers were any good was another matter. Someone on a mountain? 'High life'. Anything to do with Carlisle's Pirelli tyre factory? 'Tread carefully'.

I remembered a sub telling me that, at a previous paper, he and his colleagues had a competition to see who could write the most boring headline on the community news page. 'Gatepost painted' held the title for many years until he took it with a report of a coffee morning: 'Coffee poured'.

A sub who had worked on the sports desk used to write 'Net gain' as a kicker for stories about tennis, badminton and squash. After several years, someone broke the news to him that there's no net in squash.

Writers were also expected to take pictures when our one remaining photographer was unavailable. Reporters took pictures on their phones of defendants outside court: a far cry from the days when photographers had me as their getaway driver.

There was a big difference between writers' snaps and the pictures taken by professionals. I felt guilty about doing someone else's job. But that was an old-fashioned attitude in an era of multimedia journalism in which we were supposed to write, take photos and videos, sub, and put everything we did on our website and Facebook page.

Lots of pictures in our papers were now sourced from social media or Google Street View. Readers must have noticed the declining standard. They were encouraged to send in their own pictures, as were businesses, charities and anyone else who wouldn't charge us.

I found it hard to escape the feeling that Newsquest didn't care about journalism. *Hold the Front Page* – a website with excellent coverage of the UK's local press – quoted our regional managing director David Coates saying of another Newsquest paper, the *Northern Echo* in Darlington, 'Hopefully . . . we'll be able to move into accommodation that's more befitting a modern digital marketing services business.' Not a newspaper: a marketing services business.

Newsquest's attitude to features was summed up by a reader survey in the *News & Star*. This had thirty-two questions about what people read and what they wanted to read. The only mention of features or columns was a question asking readers to rank the *News & Star* on whether it had 'relevant lifestyle, fashion and beauty features'.

Those weren't the kind of features I wrote. They weren't the kind that Mark Green and Stephen Blease wrote either. We were the remaining three feature writers: an increasingly endangered species. *Hold the Front Page* regularly ran stories about other

Newsquest titles making redundancies. These often included any feature writers. The company's focus on the internet didn't help our prospects.

When the takeover happened, we were told that Newsquest thought CN Group had put stories online too early every day, to the detriment of its papers. Now the priority was stabilising newspaper sales. A few months later this changed: it was all about web hits again.

Every month Newsquest emailed its staff a list of the most-watched videos on its sites. The Brighton-based *Argus* did well, with clips from Facebook, or sent in by readers. These included '"Irish Gypsy" threatens the Disco Bunny' and 'Sex act in Worthing'. I didn't think sex happened in Worthing. No wonder people were curious about it.

This was a blurred-out video of a blow job on a bench in the town centre. That and the Disco Bunny were watched by many more people than read my features. Good journalism now meant trawling social media to find mobile-phone clips of fights in supermarkets. Good journalism was putting a celebrity's name in a headline so that lots of people clicked on the story. Good journalism was putting a Press Association weather warning online before any other paper, so that people searching for it would read it on your website.

Journalists who did these things were lauded by Newsquest managers. I resented that. I heard managers argue that those web hits paid for my job. But even now, after years of neglect – even with its vastly diminished sales and advertising revenue – around the country print was bringing in much more money than digital.

By the end of 2018, digital still accounted for less than 40 per cent of Newsquest's advertising revenue. Then there was the money from newspaper sales, which had no online equivalent.

I assumed the company was just too far down the digital road to turn back.

It was easy to see why Newsquest would be drawn to digital. No ink or paper to pay for. No printers or delivery drivers. Bringing the company closer to what seemed to be its dream: employing just advertising sales staff and one (part-time) trainee to write and sub its two-hundred-plus newspapers and magazines.

The gulf between the effort I put into my stories and the reward in terms of web hits was frustrating. In one week I wrote two stories that fared very differently online. I spent hours crafting a profile of an author. Then I spent ten minutes rewriting a press release about a former footballer's hair transplant. The author profile had one of the lowest numbers of hits any of my stories ever received. The footballer press release had one of the biggest numbers: 125 times more than the profile I'd slaved over.

When weeping over figures such as those, I couldn't help wondering whether features were worth writing. What kept me going was the growing conviction that our online and newspaper audiences were now different and that longer pieces were appreciated by newspaper readers.

Our newspaper readers' demographic hit home when I wrote a feature about a bowling green. I was recognised by most people there. I kept hearing my name being mentioned, and nearly choked on all the Werther's Originals I was offered. This was my public: grey-haired and no-haired. Some might see this ageing audience as a sign that Newsquest was right to prioritise digital. The fact remained that newspapers still made a lot more money.

But I feared for their future. In 2015 we covered Storm Desmond superbly, with seventeen writers and eight photographers across north and west Cumbria. How would we tackle such a huge story now?

I thought of Michael Knighton's final days at Carlisle United, when he threatened to close the club down. Like a football club, a newspaper is a community asset as well as a business. Owners can cherish them or run them into the ground.

CN Group thought that serving its communities was important. The papers declined towards the end of Robin Burgess's tenure but they weren't wilfully dismantled. Newsquest's cost-cutting business model was good for its shareholders. It was less good for communities left with hollowed-out versions of their newspapers.

Some people will always buy their local paper or read its website, if only through habit. Some businesses will always advertise with the paper or website to reach those people. With big publishers' running costs cut to the bone, there was still profit to be had. American media analyst Ken Doctor told the *New York Times*, 'The truth is, to make a huge profit in the newspaper business, you have to cut, cut, cut, and be willing to see the product get worse year by year.'

Around the UK, although not yet in Cumbria, another way was emerging. Independent weekly papers and websites had launched in towns where papers run by the big publishing groups had closed or become horribly diminished. These so-called hyperlocals were often staffed by journalists who'd been made redundant from the papers they were competing against or replacing. They ran without the big groups' thirst for big profits, and were increasingly appreciated by readers.

17

Star Wars

I SAW comedian Stewart Lee perform in Carlisle. He said, 'They say you play Carlisle twice in your career: once on the way up, and once on the way down. Anyway . . . it's great to be back.'

Many of the celebrities I interviewed were on the way down. If they'd been travelling in the opposite direction, I probably wouldn't have known about them. If they were at their peak they probably wouldn't have been performing in Cumbria.

When interviewing famous people on the downward slope I tried to ask, as subtly as possible, how it felt to be past their commercial prime. I didn't do this to try and wind them up, although some seemed to take it that way. I was fascinated by how it must feel to have sold out arenas and had chart-topping records – they were usually musicians – and to have seen those days disappear.

Eighties pop stars were my speciality. Phil Oakey of the Human League said, 'It looked like we were going to be the local joke. We always stayed in Sheffield and we could see people saying, "He used to be on *Top of the Pops*," hoping we'd sign on at the dole office. I know that isn't important, but it feels like it is.'

Former Marillion singer Fish was philosophical. 'It's kind of difficult. "Kayleigh" and "Lavender" are the two biggest songs I've ever written, far outstripping anything in my solo career, so of course people are going to talk about them.'

Others seemed in denial. I spoke to Toyah in 2009, twenty-four years after her last hit single. I thought I'd found a super-subtle way of phrasing the 'How does it feel to not be in the charts any more?' question. I asked if she ever felt frustrated that her recent work was less widely known than the music she made in her youth. She heard this as 'How does it feel to be completely past it?'

'That's not true,' she replied, with a touch of frost. 'My last album went to number six in the iTunes chart. I'm in a band with the drummer from R.E.M.'

Some performers had no choice but to acknowledge that their glory days were behind them. Bay City Rollers singer Les McKeown couldn't really have argued that his upcoming gig at Whitehaven Civic Hall was a step up from the years when he fronted one of the biggest bands in the world.

Now fifty-six, he recalled running up ramps on to stages, hearing thousands of screaming girls. He talked about the break-up, drink and drugs, missing money, and his first ever Pilates class. Our phone interview took place while he was waiting to do it. 'I've got a bit of a back issue,' he said. 'And I've got type 2 diabetes. I started going to the gym. After about five minutes on the treadmill I thought, "Christ, I'm really unfit."' He laughed, well aware that this wasn't the young man who broke hearts around the world.

With Belinda Carlisle, I tried to claim that some unspecified other people wanted to ask about her past – not me. 'Is it frustrating when you're fifty and all people want to talk about is what you did in your twenties and thirties?'

'Some questions are tired and old,' she replied. 'I prefer to talk about right now.'

I scratched a line through the long list of questions I'd written under the heading 'Heaven Is a Place on Earth'.

Belinda was performing at Whitehaven. I thought she'd want to reminisce about her gig a few years earlier in the city that shares her surname. Instead she said, 'I don't remember it. After a while these things have a tendency to blur into one.'

I scratched a line through the long list of questions I'd written under the heading 'How excited were you about performing in Carlisle?'

Celebrities were more likely than civilians to be prickly. (I'm not counting vox-pop civilians: no one was pricklier than them.) Maybe it was the realisation that they'd played stadiums and were now talking to a local paper in Cumbria. Maybe it was being asked the same questions dozens of times in a day of phone interviews. When a musician or comedian is going on tour their agent will arrange these, generally scheduled for about fifteen minutes each. Perhaps it isn't much fun to spend hours repeatedly saying the same things. Then again, I did that with my colleagues every day and it didn't put me in a bad mood.

One interview with a famous actress went well. I'd rung her at home rather than receiving a call from her agent's office. When writing up my notes next day, I found that I'd forgotten to ask an important question. Ringing a celebrity back was normally impossible. But as I had her number . . .

I rang her, and quickly wished I hadn't. She was annoyed: 'Please don't call unless it's been scheduled through my agent.' I haven't named her here in case this story makes her sound like a diva. The fault was mine, for assuming a familiarity that didn't exist. I wouldn't have expected most people to behave as she did. But celebrities are different, because the public and the media treat them that way. We can't give them special status and then be surprised when they don't behave like the man or woman in the street.

The challenges when interviewing celebrities include the wealth of background material that's already out there. I often found myself drowning in information, struggling with what to include and what to leave out. After speaking to BRIT Award-winning singer Beth Orton, I included everything I could find about her because our interview was so short. I'd rung her on her mobile. She was in Paris.

'Sorry,' she said. 'It's not a good time. I think my bag's just been stolen. It's got everything in it, my passport and purse.'

That was followed by a muffled conversation as Beth talked to someone about her bag: 'We were in that fish restaurant. Was it under my chair?'

The only question of mine that she answered was whether her work is becoming more organic. 'It's always been organic! I never use labels like that. I just make music.'

Her next and final comment before she hung up was 'I can't really talk right now. I've just lost my purse. I've lost everything! Hang on . . . I've got to go!'

It's just occurred to me that maybe Beth Orton starts every phone interview claiming to have lost her bag. If the journalist asks a good first question, the bag turns up and the interview proceeds. If they ask whether her work is becoming more organic, she has to return to an imaginary fish restaurant.

Another challenge was whether to ask celebrities about any controversies. If it was something long ago that had no direct relevance to now, I'd sometimes leave it. This could be out of respect for them, or just because some days mentioning it seemed like too much hassle.

I interviewed Marti Pellow of Wet Wet Wet about a musical he was starring in. This was years after his heroin addiction. The email from his PR people asked that the interview concentrated on the show with nothing about his personal life, which suggested that drugs remained a touchy subject.

I decided it would be unfair to say, 'Tell me about the musical, Marti. Oh, and what was life like when you were on smack?' So I didn't mention it, but I did refer to it in my feature. This now seems a cowardly compromise, like being nice to his face then talking about his dark times behind his back.

One of the biggest perks of my job was speaking to famous people I admired. If a favourite musician, comedian or writer was coming to Cumbria, I'd email their website or agent and be talking to them within a few days. Interviewing authors and comedians was like having a personal performance.

Talking to someone who'd been a star during my childhood was always strange. I'd watched this person on TV, heard them on the radio – the soundtrack to my youth and all that – and now I was having a conversation with them. That was especially surreal and nerve-wracking with a huge star like Rod Stewart. He was promoting his concert at Brunton Park. It was arranged that he'd ring me one afternoon. Well, his agent would ring me and say, 'I'm putting you across to Rod. You've got ten minutes.'

He was chatty, easy to interview, and unimpressed with having performed the biggest gig in history: to three-and-a-half million people at Rio de Janeiro. 'It was too big. I didn't enjoy it. I remember when we played the last note. We finished with "Da Ya Think I'm Sexy?" As we went off stage, the people on the beach were still hearing the last few bars.'

My nerves usually eased when an interview started. However famous they were, it was still just a case of asking them stuff and writing down what they said. With John Hurt, my nerves grew.

I'd been off sick with a nasty case of norovirus . . . I don't think anyone has ever had a nice case of norovirus. On my first day back, I'd just sat down when the features editor said, 'Can you ring John Hurt in an hour?' He was soon to be the guest of honour at Keswick Film Festival.

It felt like one of those dreams in which you've done no revision for an imminent exam. 'You have one hour to research the fifty-year career of one of the world's greatest actors and work out what to ask them.'

The interview was similar to how I imagine a psychotic episode might feel. When such a familiar voice as John Hurt's responded to what I was saying, it was like talking to the TV and hearing the actors talk back. My delicate condition heightened the sense of unreality. I'd lost half a stone in two days and was weak and light-headed. Maybe my not-quite-with-it-ness helps to explain why he seemed impatient with me.

> The journey has been made with a tuneful, rounded voice which can snap with authority when the role demands it, or when the actor is asked a question he regards as rather lame. Has his voice been much of an asset? 'You're asking me questions you already know the answer to.'

Oh God . . . I feel faint, and the Elephant Man thinks I'm an idiot. Thankfully he said interesting things, even while annoyed.

> See Hurt immersed in a role and you wonder if the performance is a tribute to his training, or whether the ability to act is simply either there or not. 'You're asking me that as if I'm some sort of prophet who knows the answers. If you have a talent, you can improve it. If you

have a blade with an edge on, you can sharpen it. I'm not sure you can make an edge if there isn't one.'

At the end of the interview, sweaty and dry-mouthed, I resorted to asking what it was like when the creature erupted from his stomach in *Alien*. He probably reckoned I thought *Alien* was a documentary. By that stage I couldn't be sure either way.

In terms of his career trajectory, Rodney Bewes was the acting equivalent of Les McKeown. *The Likely Lads* star was performing a solo version of *Three Men in a Boat*. He rang newspapers himself to arrange interviews and drove between theatres in his twelve-year-old Ford Mondeo, towing the scenery in a trailer.

He was happy to discuss *The Likely Lads*, even though he'd filmed it decades earlier. 'There's a DVD box set. When I get cheques I don't complain. If someone criticises something they get money for, they should get a kick. I'm very lucky to be remembered for something good. A lot of actors are remembered for rubbish.'

He was a great interviewee, self-deprecatingly funny and admirably enthusiastic. I asked if he ever felt like retiring. 'Never. I want to die on stage. As an old butler. I've got a tray of glasses. I say "Your sherry, my lord." Then I fall. All the glasses hit the ground with a crash. "Aarrghh!" Slow curtain.'

I thought I'd reached peak celebrity in 2008 during a phone interview with Chas, of Chas and Dave. David Cameron, then Leader of the Opposition and two years from becoming Prime Minister, walked into the newsroom, for reasons I can't remember.

'David Cameron's just walked in,' I told Chas.

'Oh, right,' said Chas.

'It's celebrity overload!' I said. 'It's Chas and David!'

'Yeah, right,' said Chas.

I didn't speak to David Cameron. But I did ask Chas if people got him and Dave mixed up. He said they did. 'I answer to both names. I was at a festival last week and this woman came up to me and said, "Hello, Dave." Dave was at the other end of the room so I just said, "Yeah, hello." Then when Dave came over, I introduced him as Chas.'

There were even greater celebrity heights ahead. Three years later I travelled to Blackpool for the opening of the town's Comedy Carpet. This vast piece of public art on the pavement opposite Blackpool Tower features jokes and catchphrases by many of Britain's best-loved comedians. It was created by Cumbrian artist Gordon Young, hence my presence.

The launch really was celebrity overload, largely thanks to kids' TV stars from yesteryear. My interviewees included the Krankies and the Chuckle Brothers. The main attraction was Ken Dodd. I hoped for more than a quick word with Ken, which meant waiting for the scrum of national TV, radio and newspaper reporters to interview him. Eventually I was the only journalist left. As he ambled towards the tower I introduced myself and he agreed to a chat, even though there wasn't much in it for him. He'd played in Carlisle not long before so an interview with me wasn't going to sell him any tickets.

Ken makes his way back into the tower, down gloomy corridors to the staff lift. A middle-aged woman beams when she sees him. A little boy shelters behind his mother's legs when Ken waves his tickling stick.

We drank tea in the ballroom as the organist played. It felt like a great interview. Reading it back, it wasn't. Part of me regrets that

I didn't enjoy interviews more. But wherever I was and whoever I talked with, it was work. I concentrated on what they were saying, writing it down, wondering what to ask next.

With Ken Dodd, I enjoyed the interview too much. I relaxed at the end of a long day, thought how pleasant it was to be sipping tea with this legend, and didn't ask good enough questions. Ken had performed a brief routine at the Comedy Carpet's official opening a few hours earlier and was still brilliant, a month from his eighty-fourth birthday. In our interview he was on cruise control and I was having too nice a time to notice. That can happen with celebrities. It could seem like what they were saying was fascinating, just because these words were coming from a famous mouth.

Ken's answers were still good. But later I realised that I'd got more from him in a phone interview the previous year, before one of his shows in Carlisle. That was my stab at 'Who is the real Ken Dodd behind the jester's mask?' He said, 'There's no puzzle there. I'm just a mainstream comedian. If you start psychoanalysing entertainers you're bound to find a lot of paradoxes. We're human, after all. I think that's part of the reason you become an entertainer . . .'

At that moment I thought I was on the verge of a revelation, the funny man finally revealing his motivation. And maybe he did. 'You become an entertainer because you want to tickle a lot of people. It's a lovely feeling. The sound of laughter is the most beautiful sound in the world. Better than any symphony orchestra.'

Famous Cumbrians is a club so small that when I searched for that phrase, Google suggested, 'Do you mean famous Colombians?' I'd interview Melvyn Bragg when he'd written a new book or when a new series of *The South Bank Show* was starting. He was always friendly, as was Helen Skelton when we spoke about her adventures such as kayaking the Amazon and trekking to the South Pole.

I once interviewed Helen at the *Blue Peter* studio in Salford. I was pleased that the BBC had moved its children's unit to the north. But would it have killed them to wait until I'd had the chance to visit the *Blue Peter* studio I'd grown up watching at Television Centre in London?

Lee Brennan, the singer with 1990s boy band 911, is the only Cumbrian to have had a chart-topping single. He gave me some great interviews about the rise and fall of a pop star.

I've failed to get many potentially intriguing interviews, at least one of which involved a Cumbrian. Roxanne Pallett is from Carlisle. In 2018 the former *Emmerdale* actress became infamous for her stint on *Celebrity Big Brother*. After falsely accusing actor Ryan Thomas of punching her, she was described in the media as the most-hated woman in Britain. She left the Big Brother house and went into hiding.

I'd interviewed Roxanne several times, kind of. There'd been one phone interview soon after she joined *Emmerdale*. In the years since she left the programme I'd tried for others when she was appearing on stage or in TV shows. Her management always asked me to email questions. That request was occasionally made when I tried to interview other celebrities. What came back sometimes bore little relation to what I'd asked. It was mainly just comments promoting their latest project.

Roxanne's answers were always penned in response to my questions, with lots of references to people and places in Carlisle. They were well-written and informative. But I thought that sending her responses in writing was a sign that she had issues with trust and liked to be in control. Admittedly, I cobbled together this theory only after *Celebrity Big Brother*. I looked at all her answers again for clues to her behaviour in the house. There was none that I could see. And our pen-pal relationship proved worthless when I joined countless other journalists in not getting an interview.

Gregor Fisher, who plays Rab C. Nesbitt, used to live in the Scottish Borders. One day I saw him in Carlisle city centre. 'Hello, Gregor? I'm a journalist with the *Cumberland News*.'

'I'm very sorry.'

I asked if he'd be up for an interview some time. He took my notebook, wrote down his agent's details and told me to contact them. A day or two later I looked for what he'd written and couldn't find it. I went through every page of the book. There was no sign. Months later it occurred to me that maybe he had a pen with disappearing ink and used it for hilarious pranks such as winding up journalists. I can't think of any other explanation.

The interview never happened. For years I googled 'Gregor Fisher agent' but couldn't find any details. I've just googled 'Gregor Fisher agent' and their name came up immediately. I may be going mad.

In 2019 Colin Firth and Stanley Tucci were in the Lake District to make a film called *Supernova*. I tracked the crew to a diner on the A66. The producer said she'd rather I didn't interview the stars while filming was going on. I agreed to hold off for a few weeks until the end of the shoot, when she'd try to get me a chat with them.

Later that day the production's PR manager rang me. An interview was very unlikely, he said, but he'd send me a press release when the shoot was over. To make myself feel better I made a token protest, saying I'd been (half) promised an interview. He said he would try to get me one. We both knew it wouldn't happen.

I could have threatened to reveal filming locations in our papers, which would have attracted crowds and made the shoot more difficult, if I didn't get an interview. But much as I'd have liked to speak to the stars, I liked not being a prick even more. And the truth was that we needed them more than they needed us, even if all we were getting was a press release when they'd gone back home.

One morning I saw how desperate some people are to be famous. *The X Factor* was holding auditions in Carlisle. This event was less glamorous than might have been expected. The auditions took place in the city centre, in a tent erected by the four *X Factor* production staff who were also judging.

I spoke to some of those waiting for their moment, and tried to speak to them afterwards. That wasn't always possible. Most hurried away after being rejected. I wondered why many of those auditioning were putting themselves through this: the middle-aged and the elderly who had as much chance of winning *The X Factor* as I had of winning Miss World. One was auditioning for the fifth time. When does following your dream turn into a sad delusion?

The queue warmed up by singing 'Reach for the Stars'. One man muttered that 'Tragedy' would be more appropriate. Some auditionees could be heard from outside, warbling like Mariah Carey. A bystander said to me of a woman inside, 'I think she just blew the roof off the tent.'

That expression has stayed with me. It deserves to be widely used. I've imagined Simon Cowell gushing to a successful contestant, 'You know what? *You just blew the roof off the tent!*' Cue a standing ovation and tears of joy.

Perhaps the royal family are the most enduring celebrities of all.

I can't remember the last time any of them had a hit single or a decent film role, but they never go out of fashion.

In 2002 the Queen came to Carlisle as part of her Golden Jubilee. In one sense, covering royal visits is easy. The pressure is off because you know you're not going to interview them. If the Queen had suddenly said, 'What would one like to ask one?' I'd have crapped myself. But all I needed to do was describe the scene and ask some of those in the crowd just how radiant they thought she was looking.

Prince Charles visited Carlisle's Pirelli factory for its fiftieth anniversary. Employees queued to meet him. Journalists were shepherded around by a PR lady who told us where to stand. It reminded me of Jordan in that nightclub: someone being treated differently just because they're famous. Charles didn't offer to sit on my lap though. He was too busy performing the classic royal duty of pointing at things and asking what they are.

Sophie, Countess of Wessex, visited Carlisle Mencap. A news editor asked me to film some video on my mobile. There were spells, under both CN Group and Newsquest, when we were told it was vital to put videos on our website. For reasons no one was able to explain, stories with video brought in more money than stories without video.

My attempt to squeeze to the front of the press photographers' pack was not entirely successful. If we'd used any of my shaky footage, filmed from behind a large plant, I could have been arrested on suspicion of stalking.

Terry Waite and Simon Weston would probably rather not be household names. Terry spent nearly five years as a hostage in Lebanon, having gone there to secure the release of hostages on behalf of the Church of England. He recalled facing a mock execution. 'The gun was put to my head. I thought it was the end.' He felt strangely calm. Then his captor lowered the gun and said, 'Another time.'

In 2012 Terry returned to Lebanon to meet some of the men who had held him prisoner more than twenty years earlier. 'I believe this: we'll never have a political settlement unless people on the ground are able to really put the past in the past and begin to relate to each other as human beings rather than combatants.'

Simon Weston had similarly hard-won wisdom. Having suffered appalling burns as a young soldier in the Falklands War, he later became friends with the Argentine fighter pilot who launched the bombs that maimed him and killed forty-eight of his comrades. 'The fact that Carlos and myself are very good friends is something of note,' he said, in a south Wales rumble. 'He was doing his job and I was doing mine. He just managed to do his job better than me. He was a target, the same as I was. He's a very kind and compassionate man.' ·

I interviewed Simon and Terry in 2015. This was a time of increasing division as the Brexit debate and Donald Trump's presidential campaign intensified. Meanwhile, these two men who talked about the importance of tolerance knew a lot about its absence.

18

The Incredible Shrinking Staff List

WITHIN weeks of starting at CN Group in 1995, I joined the NUJ. The arrival of my first press card – which bore my photo and described me as a 'bona fide news gatherer' – was a proud moment, even though I couldn't have gathered news unless it had been rounded up and brought to my desk by a sheepdog.

Almost all Carlisle editorial staff were in the NUJ. Every autumn our union representative would talk to CN's management about next year's pay rise. In my early days there was always a pay rise. Even during the boom years managers would argue that times were hard, before agreeing to an increase of around 2 or 3 per cent.

Newsquest was notoriously reluctant to give pay rises. According to the NUJ, at the time of the takeover many of its staff had received just two in the past eleven years. Unlike CN, Newsquest didn't allow union meetings on its premises. Instead of having them in a room in the back corridor, we arranged them at a charity ten minutes' walk away. We once met at Carlisle City Council's HQ, at its leader's invitation. He said that he didn't always like what we wrote, but he appreciated the importance of local journalism.

Our pay had barely risen in a decade. Most of that barren spell wasn't down to Newsquest. But we'd sympathised with Robin Burgess's situation. In contrast, Newsquest made huge profits. It felt important to tell the company that we weren't prepared to keep seeing our pay eroded while our workloads expanded because they'd made so many of our colleagues redundant.

There'd always been times when we worked extra hours unpaid to cover a big story. Now there was an unspoken feeling among some managers and reporters that this was an everyday part of the job. Leaving the newsroom on time when there were still gaps to be filled in next day's paper was seen by some as letting colleagues down. My conscience wasn't troubled by leaving eight hours after I'd arrived. Giving free labour to a company that made massive profits didn't really appeal. If I wanted to do voluntary work, I'd do it for a charity.

Having said all that, I didn't exactly stride out of the newsroom every afternoon with a cheery, 'So long, losers!' From my early forties I'd started waking earlier and coming to work earlier, normally 7 to 8 a.m. Leaving between 3 and 4 p.m. felt a tad awkward when most people hadn't seen me arrive and naturally assumed I was taking the piss. I'd try and shuffle out unnoticed. As I touched the door handle, someone would inevitably shout, 'See you tomorrow!' I'd wince and think, *Was there any need for that?*

In the previous few years, many of our best reporters had left because they couldn't afford to stay. They loved journalism but couldn't face spending the rest of their careers seeing their pay diminish while working ever-more unpaid overtime.

Our NUJ branch issued a statement about the departures, the pay freeze and Newsquest's reluctance to negotiate. 'The net result has been a steady and continuous loss of our most experienced local journalists. On this evidence, we can only conclude that Newsquest Cumbria in the long term is likely to be staffed primarily by transient, overworked, underpaid journalists, who are either trainees or recently qualified. This will clearly help the firm to keep its costs down, but it will not secure a safe, viable business for the future.'

Concerns about pay and the declining quality of our papers led us to vote for a one-day strike. It would be the first by our journalists since the 1980s. On the day the strike was called, the president of Newsquest's American parent company Gannett announced that he was retiring. As part of a transition plan, he would receive $435,000 each month for the following five months. If he made it through the transition period, he'd get a million-dollar bonus.

The NUJ's warning that experienced staff were leaving was unlikely to trouble Newsquest. Many of us thought the company would be glad to have them off the payroll. Newsquest employed apprentices, one of them in Carlisle. In their first year they earned £7,250. That worked out at £27.88 per working day. In my trial period twenty-three years earlier, I was paid £30 a day.

The strike took place five days before Christmas, 2018. The law dictated that we give the company two weeks' notice: time enough for it to squirrel away material. We weren't trying to stop the papers coming out. We were sending a message to Newsquest, and to the public who probably had no idea about the extent of staff cuts and pay erosion.

The strike was well supported. Politicians and even an archdeacon joined our picket line. Local TV and radio stations covered it. Their journalists were sympathetic: BBC and ITV had suffered cuts at local level. Passing cars honked support. No keyboard warriors took the chance to offer their opinions in person.

The *Hold the Front Page* and *Press Gazette* websites reported the strike and included a picture of the pickets. I was holding a placard saying 'Local news matters'. I couldn't find one that said 'Local features matter'.

We'd have been amazed if the strike had persuaded Newsquest to give us a pay rise. This was an opponent on whom conventional weapons didn't work. But it was satisfying to make a stand, to receive support and to feel camaraderie with former colleagues, journalists from our Workington and Whitehaven sister papers, and other NUJ members who travelled from further afield.

We were docked a day's pay, so NUJ branches around the country clubbed together for us. We each got £50. The apprentice nearly doubled his daily rate.

When its accounts were published, it turned out that Newsquest had enjoyed a decent 2018. The company made pre-tax profits of £108 million. CEO Henry Faure Walker received a package of £526,204, plus pension payments of £17,260. Some pay freeze.

The following month, ten months after the takeover, Newsquest proposed giving us new contracts. We were still on CN Group's terms and conditions. Newsquest's proposals included slashing the time that staff could receive full sick pay. We were told the changes were to align our contracts with those of other Newsquest employees, and to give us access to 'the range of company benefits' available to all employees. These benefits were never revealed, at least not to me.

We pointed out that over the years a handful of staff in desperate situations had been helped by CN's sick-pay terms. They included people with cancer and a woman who nearly died in a car crash.

The NUJ suggested that Newsquest was trying to impose the changes rather than have the meaningful consultation required by law. The company then suggested reducing sick pay by a smaller amount. We agreed to that while continuing to resist some other proposals, such as removing a day's holiday and ending time-and-a-half for working bank holidays. Newsquest accepted this, for the moment, saying it would be looked at again the following year. That summer the company gave Carlisle editorial a 2 per cent pay rise. We knew it could well afford this. But the move was appreciated, and needed.

***

The newsroom was emptier. Most of my friends had gone. One of them used to ring me from across the room to whinge about the world. Sometimes he'd just call me a wanker and hang up. I missed that.

At lunchtime I'd often be the only person in the canteen, with just my tuna and sweetcorn sandwiches for company. Many of those who remained didn't take a lunch break, eating at their desks instead.

Our business, crime, politics, education and health reporters were among those who'd left without being replaced. Every few months another reporter departed, mostly for PR jobs with businesses or public bodies. Cumbria had far more PR people than journalists. They sent us press releases. Too often these were published with no time to check them, or even consider if they were worth using.

That rarely happened when we had more staff. If a press release had suggested a story worth telling, it would be rewritten and expanded with fresh quotes. Raw press releases can be like untreated sewage. People I'd interviewed – down-to-earth straight talkers – were apparently now using phrases such as 'transformational change' and words like 'upskill'. There seemed no need for businesses to advertise when they were guaranteed free publicity by sending us a few hundred words and a picture about their beer promotion or their new manager.

One reporter left for a PR job after more than twenty years. On her last day she took pictures of the sparsely populated newsroom and the deserted reception area. She told me her husband said they reminded him of photos of Chernobyl after the disaster.

People would ring up and say, 'Can I talk to someone in your arts department?' or 'Can I speak to your fashion reporter?' I resisted the urge to ask if they were taking the piss.

I thought about how lively the building used to be. A few years earlier it was buzzing from 8 a.m. For the next two hours the front few pages and the back page were still being written and subbed. Then downstairs the presses would rumble. Now everything was finished by ten the night before and the papers were printed a hundred miles away. When I came in, there'd be just one or two others in the newsroom. Even as the day went on there was only ever a fraction of the staff we used to have.

I found a list of internal phone numbers from 2008, just before the first wave of redundancies. Staff numbers then had fallen since the 1990s, but only slightly. In the Carlisle newsroom this document listed sixteen reporters, five feature writers, two sports writers, sixteen sub-editors, three sports subs and five photographers. There were also department heads and deputies, and several editorial assistants: a total of sixty-four people, plus more in our west Cumbria offices. A decade later, we had about one third that amount.

Sixty-four seemed a ridiculous number now. But those people had produced a daily tabloid with three editions (east Cumbria, west Cumbria and a Late Final for Carlisle city centre), a weekly broadsheet with numerous supplements and editions, a free weekly paper – the *Gazette* – and various other supplements. The *Gazette* and the Late Final editions of the *News & Star* and the *Cumberland News* had been scrapped. But now we had the website to feed.

The number of feature writers that we used to have had become a subject of debate. This was used as a benchmark for how much cash had been swilling around in the good old days. People would say, 'Do you remember when we had X feature writers?' – 'X' being a large number.

The most I heard anyone claim was ten. I was relieved to find those extension numbers and see that we had five. Plenty, yes. But we filled a big chunk of the papers and their supplements with in-depth pieces requiring lots of research and interviews.

We three remaining feature writers felt increasingly vulnerable. As the number of reporters declined, the features department began to look disproportionately large. Three was certainly more feature writers than most local papers had. In many cases, three more.

My sense of living on borrowed time was fuelled both by feature writers being seen as a luxury and a feeling of being in a dying industry: a twenty-first-century lamplighter. Local journalism was becoming a place for people younger and cheaper than me. Most of those who remained were in their twenties. I was pushing fifty, and feeling like their grandfather. My ageing process was on fast-forward. In three years I went from being younger than average to one of the oldest in the newsroom.

Any new recruits were trainees. There was also the apprentice, who envied trainees' modest salaries. And around the country the BBC paid for 150 local democracy reporters (LDRs), who also tended to be young. LDRs were employed by regional news organisations to cover the work of councils and other public bodies. The BBC agreed to fund them as a condition of its charter; a useful response to accusations that its website harmed local papers.

Newsquest had several LDRs, some in Cumbria. The vast majority were placed with the big three local newspaper groups: Newsquest, Reach and JPI Media. The NUJ accused big publishers of, in some cases, laying off journalists then employing those paid for by licence-fee payers. Stephen Kingston, editor of hyperlocal magazine *Salford Star*, told *Hold the Front Page*, 'The news groups that have benefited from BBC funding have been sacking journalists for years in the relentless pursuit of more profit.' By 2018, LDRs made up about 5 per cent of Newsquest's editorial staff. The company praised the scheme and called for its expansion.

In Carlisle we also employed one of the eighty trainee journalists who were funded for two years by a £4.5 million donation to the newspaper industry from Facebook. Much of Facebook's and Google's vast profits came from people viewing, sharing and searching for journalism on their platforms.

As readers increasingly used Facebook and Google to read journalists' work, businesses moved their advertising from newspaper websites to the tech giants. In the decade to 2017, the share of the UK advertising market going to newspapers fell from almost half to just over 10 per cent.

That year *Press Gazette* launched a campaign urging Facebook and Google to make 'a fairer deal with the news industry'. A comment piece noted that advertising revenue, which used to fund journalists holding those in power to account, 'has been transferred to two US-owned digital platforms which exist purely to exploit content rather than create it'.

Press Gazette made it clear that newspapers were not the only media suffering. 'Channel 4 News has generated literally billions of video views for Facebook – much of it for work created at great personal risk by journalists working inside Syria. By way of financial return it gets almost nothing, while Facebook banks the advertising income. Facebook profits while others take the risks and responsibility.'

In 2018 the News Media Association, the British newspaper industry's trade body, expressed its concern for 'the loss of advertising revenues which have previously sustained quality national and local journalism and are now flowing to the global search engines and social media companies who make no meaningful contribution to the cost of producing the original content from which they so richly benefit.'

Newsquest's CEO Henry Faure Walker thought Facebook and Google should give something back. I agreed. I didn't blame the big newspaper groups for all the industry's problems. CN Group was already in such a downward spiral, it might not have survived much longer if a larger company hadn't bought it.

By the time of the takeover, the industry had been devastated by years of advertising revenue disappearing and years of giving away its product online: a product that now consisted largely of press releases and reader-submitted photos. Newsquest had the resources to improve CN's papers and websites. But its strategy seemed to be to cut costs enough every year to still make a profit. You can do that for only so long until there's nothing left to cut.

Newsquest might not have been notably worse than the other big local newspaper publishers. All were partial to making staff redundant. All were searching for a solution that may not have existed. Newsquest demanded that we slow the decline in newspaper sales, while insisting that we put even more stories online.

The message that everything should go on our website was reinforced daily. Every story, however small. Every columnist. Even the horoscopes. I'd think, please, can you leave people with *some* reason to buy the paper?

Digital came with its own jargon, most of which made my ears bleed. Instead of 'Will you time that story to go on the website at nine tomorrow morning?' news editors started saying, 'Will you time-bomb that story for nine tomorrow morning?' The first time I heard this, I looked around the newsroom. Everyone seemed to have a straight face. Had they all gone mad? It sounded like something from *Doctor Who*. I imagined Davros screaming, 'Unleash . . . THE TIME BOMB!'

Time-bombing lasted a few months before sanity was restored and stories were merely timed. But Newsquest bosses sent us regular emails about Chartbeat. To this day I have no idea what Chartbeat is. And we kept hearing about something called CrowdTangle. Eventually a colleague turned to me and asked, 'What *is* CrowdTangle?'

'I have no idea.'

He shook his head. 'CrowdTangle . . . it sounds like a fucking *Worzel Gummidge* character.'

Newsquest advertised for an audience and content editor. The advert began with the words, 'Is story-telling your passion? Do you know your CrowdTangle from your Chartbeat?' I didn't apply.

***

The North West Media Awards 2018. My twelfth time on the shortlist. Finally, I won. Disbelief and joy had a party in my head. *Hold the Front Page* ran a story about my long-awaited triumph. One reader commented, 'Well done him, but I have worked with some brilliant journos who never went near awards competitions. They never needed their egos massaging, though no doubt this young man is very modest.' If only.

A logo was designed for our papers with my picture and the name of the award. Whether by accident or design, subs always seemed to use this next to some non-award-winning brief news story I'd dashed out, such as an open day at a crematorium. The category name had changed from Feature Writer to Best Writer. That was a reflection of how few feature writers were left. Still – a trophy saying I was the best writer in the north-west. Maybe that would save me from the fate that faced all Newsquest feature writers.

19

Ordinary/Extraordinary

IN a way, celebrity interviews are interesting regardless of what's said. Rod Stewart told me that he likes Cumberland sausage. That became a *News & Star* splash. It would need to be a very slow news day for the same revelation from a civilian to make the front page.

Celebs were often going through the motions, not really revealing themselves. Ordinary people, unguarded by agents and unburned by previous interviews, were where the gold was found. In the best examples they were talking about something more compelling than singing a song or reading a script.

People could be intriguing for epic or eccentric reasons. Sometimes both. Like millions around the world, I was drawn to the grainy black-and-white footage of Donald Campbell's *Bluebird K7* lifting off Coniston Water in the Lake District, then somersaulting and crashing into it. That was 1967. Thirty-four years later a Geordie engineer and diver called Bill Smith found and raised the wreckage.

At a workshop in North Shields, Tyne and Wear, he and about a dozen volunteers were tackling the daunting task of reviving *Bluebird*'s grey skeleton so she could glide again. Bill agreed to an interview on condition that I brought a jar of coffee for the troops. He wasn't impressed by my Mellow Bird's but talked to me regardless. He was a great speaker: opinionated, resolute and surprisingly sensitive. Before retrieving the wreckage, Bill had journeyed to the lake bed. He felt he had to speak to Donald Campbell and tell him that his daughter Gina supported the project to raise *Bluebird* and its pilot.

> I got it into my daft head that we should go to the bottom and tell him what was going on. We ended up building this lighting tower, positioned over the site. I'm slowly sinking to the bottom in all this brilliant light. Donald's lying there. 'Look, Donald, we're mates. Gina sent us. She wants to take you home.'

Cedric Martindale had spent twelve years and £25,000 campaigning to have the Penrith–Keswick rail line reopened. Politicians expressed varying degrees of support but with no end product. In 1999 Cedric applied to the National Lottery's Millennium Fund, and was repeatedly asked for more detail. 'The third time, they told us we'd qualified for funding, but unfortunately there wasn't any money left. That was the week three hundred million pounds was diverted to the Millennium Dome.'

He then applied to the Heritage Lottery Fund and was told that his bid fulfilled the criteria. 'But we couldn't have the money because we didn't own the land – they turned us down because we don't own the Lake District National Park.' In 2020, twenty-four years after Cedric's campaign had begun, there was renewed hope that the line would be reopened with the help of government backing.

Tommy Little was eighty when I met him, still fit and mentally sharp. Tommy was one of several people I interviewed who had been involved in the biggest story of the past century. A natural storyteller, he would lean forward and stare straight ahead as he talked, reliving events and conversations from the Second World War in piercing detail.

On D-Day, a week before his twenty-first birthday, Tommy landed on a Normandy beach. He then spent three months chasing fleeing Germans north and became part of Operation Market Garden: the failed attempt to gain control of three Dutch bridges to pave the way for an Allied advance into Germany. The operation was immortalised in the film *A Bridge Too Far*.

That Christmas, 1944, he was in the Dutch town of Brunssum. He and some comrades were staying in a family's house. They made the offer after Tommy had given their son some much-needed food. 'That really changed my life,' Tommy told me. 'When I looked at this loving family and what they'd been through – the Gestapo had had hold of their father – I thought "Well, if you can stick it, I can stick it."'

Next spring, Tommy became one of the first British soldiers to enter Germany as Hitler's empire crumbled. The retreating Germans had no time to move their dead.

> You lived and ate and slept among dead people. Every day you saw horrible things. But then we were a lot younger in them days. We somehow just accepted what was going on as the norm. The next day was another day and you were doing other things. But when you look back from where I am now, you wonder how you lived through it. You never felt you were going to be the one that was killed. I always thought I would make it back so that I would marry Hilda.

And he did. Tommy returned to Carlisle and spent the rest of his working life as a supervisor in a textile mill. He seemed to have had a good life, albeit scarred by Hilda's death from cancer. 'That was worse than any military service. A little bit of me died with her.'

Their grandson was taking a course in music industry management. 'He knows the lasses out of Destiny's Child very well,' Tommy said.

He had another family: the family from Brunssum. The boy Tommy had shared his food with was now a grandfather. The grandchildren phoned Tommy every Christmas morning.

I interviewed Tommy about the war several times. Always happy to help me, he also became my go-to pensioner for stories about the elderly, such as how they coped with energy bills.

The first time I interviewed him he was preparing to go back to Arnhem, scene of Operation Market Garden, 'to thank the lads that lie in the ground. They had no life. I have no complaints. I had a nice lass to come home to. Those lads gave their life for our way of living.'

Just before Christmas 2010 I visited Tommy with a card. He asked if I could give him a lift into town. He was a bit more fragile than I'd seen him before. It had been snowing. When I dropped him off, he waved goodbye and trudged away in his wellies. I never saw Tommy again. He died a few months later. He was eighty-seven.

Of all the people I interviewed, it's Tommy that I think about most. He still helps me. *Well, if you can stick it, I can stick it.* I apply those words to what he went through and anything that I'm struggling with. They put my problems in perspective.

You'd never have known that this quiet old man was living history. 'It's like a dream now when I think about the war,' he said. 'I know I was there but it's hard to believe it.'

I can still picture Tommy, still hear the inflections and the rising tension as he described his younger self's struggle to stay alive. Tommy had stood shoulder to shoulder with men who were there one minute and gone the next. In the decades since, he had plenty of time to think about a brutal way of life and death. But his summary was very simple. 'Some's lucky,' he said. 'And some aren't.'

Bob Lee had been lucky and unlucky in the same moment. Another Second World War veteran, he was patrolling at Arnhem when a shell landed nearby. A lump of shrapnel blew through his back, through his right lung, deflected up through his right arm and emerged from his shoulder. Bob thought he'd been hit by a brick. He showed me the small cube of metal – dark brown, rough-edged and heavier than it looked – that nearly killed him. Instead he saw friends die and went on to live another sixty-six years.

Not every victim of war had faced enemy fire. At eighty-eight, Annie Kirkwood still mourned her first husband Harold. Like Tommy Little, Harold had landed on a Normandy beach on D-Day. But Harold was unlucky. When Annie received a letter from his commanding officer, she almost fell down the stairs in her rush to pick it up. She told me, 'I thought it was going to say he was all right. It said that his tank had been hit by an anti-tank gun and he'd been killed instantly, as soon as the tank rolled on to the beach.'

Annie described Harold as a lovely man. They'd married when she was eighteen. She sent him a card just before he died. 'I don't know if he got it or not. He wasn't a bit bothered about going into war. He went in with a good heart. He used to say to us, "I'll come back, lass. All the bad uns come back." I said, "You're not a bad un, lad."'

20

Donald Trumped by My Friend Francis

On a day off in the summer of 2018, I was at home watching a press conference held by Donald Trump and Theresa May. After reading their statements, they took questions from journalists. Theresa May gestured to one of them and said, 'Francis.' Well, she actually said 'Fraaancis.' And there on my screen was someone I hadn't seen for twenty years. When I knew Francis Elliott, he was a reporter for the *Cumberland News* and the *News & Star*. Now he was political editor of *The Times*.

My first encounter with him occurred a year before I started working at CN Group. I was taking part in a raft race in Carlisle. Francis was interviewing participants. He told my team that he didn't think our craft looked particularly river-worthy: a judgement that was vindicated when it broke in half as we clambered aboard. My friend Jonny had retorted, 'She's built for speed, not looks.'

That quote appeared in Francis's story next day. I'd been jealous of Jonny. But not as jealous as I was of Francis right now, as the British Prime Minister invited him to question the President of the United States. I watched and thought, *What the fuck have I done with my life?*

Francis asked Trump about his claim that immigration had damaged the cultural fabric of Europe. 'I think it's been very bad for Europe,' reiterated Trump, prompting a veiled reproach from May.

The following summer they held another press conference. This time Francis asked the President if he agreed that the entire UK economy, including the NHS, needed to be on the table in any UK–US trade talks. 'Everything is on the table – so, NHS or anything else,' said Trump.

Both replies made international headlines. My interviews with politicians tended to be councillors talking about bin collections.

After he joined *The Times*, I'd interviewed Francis on the phone. He insisted that journalism was the same job wherever you did it. You asked people stuff and reported what they said. Of course he was right. Still . . . I could identify with how a lower-league footballer might feel when seeing a former team-mate play for Real Madrid.

Francis wasn't the only one to excel on a bigger stage. Mark Hughes came to CN as a trainee reporter. After a few years he moved to the *Independent* then the *Daily Telegraph*, where he became news editor. Some other former colleagues were reporters at the *Sunday Mirror*, the *Sunday People* and the *Scottish Sun*.

I asked myself whether I could have made that kind of leap. Having the confidence to reach the level of interviewing prime ministers and presidents felt beyond me. Life on a local paper was enough. Another kind of supposed promotion – becoming a news or features editor – never held any appeal. You're good at interviewing and writing, so you're now going to attend meetings and plan what goes where in the paper. Success for me was to keep doing the same thing.

I was still embarrassed about my short-lived attempt to do it somewhere else. Edinburgh felt like unfinished business. At one point I tried to go back. The year 2009 had carried strange echoes of earlier times. I was seeing someone who lived in Edinburgh. We talked about me moving up there. I contacted the editor of the *Evening News* about job opportunities. Fortunately for me, the editor was no longer John McLellan. I met the new boss. He seemed to like my work and he accepted my explanation that I'd ended my first stint at the paper because there hadn't been time to write the kind of features I relished.

But John McLellan was now editor-in-chief of The Scotsman Publications Ltd's papers, including the *Evening News*. When the editor didn't contact me after our meeting, I emailed him to ask if there was any progress. He was less optimistic about my prospects than he'd been a few days earlier. I don't know if John McLellan scuppered my chances. If he did, I'd have understood. Either way, my return never happened. I could tell myself that second time around I would definitely have made it work.

21

Fancy Dress for Dogs

Newsquest's economies of scale helped it to make efficiencies, even if those largely entailed making people redundant. Some felt like false economies. The company laid off our receptionist and locked the front doors, except for 10 a.m. to 2 p.m., Monday to Friday. Reception existed mainly so that people could give us money. They bought newspapers and magazines, took out subscriptions and placed adverts. Or they tried to. Even when the building was open to the public, this was now challenging.

A bell on the reception desk occasionally summoned a reluctant member of staff from a nearby department. And there was a phone. A notice next to it listed a bewildering set of instructions, which often culminated in a recorded message, an engaged tone or a conversation with Newsquest's Bradford office, more than a hundred miles away. I wondered if the company's customer service could improve any further. Perhaps a ring of barbed wire and a crocodile pit outside the main entrance.

All this had serious implications. Colleagues returned to the newsroom describing encounters downstairs with tearful members of the public who'd been struggling to place an obituary. When passing through reception I'd see people with the phone in their hand, looking around for help. One couple's mood suggested they'd been waiting a while. They were trying to buy a magazine subscription, without success.

'Don't you want our money?' snapped the woman. Subscriptions was one of the departments listed on the notice by the phone. I followed the instructions. The line was engaged. I went back upstairs to the subscriptions department. No one was there. I came back down and tried the phone again. It was still engaged.

I apologised, gave the woman my business card and asked her to send me an email with her thoughts on the situation, which I'd forward to our regional managing director. Her email bemoaned the poor quality of service. I forwarded it as promised, and heard nothing back from the MD. I then took to using a side entrance between ten and two.

There was no escape. The lack of a receptionist meant phone calls increasingly came through to editorial from people wanting to buy a magazine or sell a fridge. At my desk I sometimes heard forlorn shouts of 'Hello?' drifting up from reception. I pretended not to hear them.

We must have lost a huge amount of custom. Then there was the damage to our reputation of so many people spreading the word that they'd come to our premises at 9 a.m. or 3 p.m. to find them locked. And if they turned up when we were open, they may have wished they hadn't. I wouldn't have minded so much if Newsquest was just ruthless. But ruthless and crap was a depressing combination.

After so many departures, the building and its vast car park were far bigger than was needed. An air of decay clung to everything. Weeds flourished between the paving slabs outside reception. In winter the heating was so unreliable that some of us worked in our coats. Buckets were placed under leaks in the roof. One afternoon, part of the ceiling collapsed in a corridor. I discovered the debris on the floor. In hindsight, my life could have been vastly improved by lying in it, screaming, and trying my hand at claiming compensation.

The handyman who for many years maintained the large, crumbling building had taken voluntary redundancy a few months earlier. People who used to be a big part of our lives were disappearing in numerous ways. Robin Burgess died in February 2019, a year to the day after Newsquest's takeover was announced. On *Hold the Front Page* his death prompted heartfelt tributes. I wrote his obituary in the *Cumberland News*, using quotes from the interview I'd conducted with him on his retirement, just three years earlier.

We'd sat in the boardroom with its wood-panelled walls and the black-and-white photographs of three previous generations of his family. His photograph would be joining them. Some people had suggested that it should be black-and-white, for continuity. 'I'm for colour,' he said. 'For progress.'

Things had certainly changed. Robin was once the centre of this universe. At six feet five inches, a huge figure in every way. Now he was a fond memory. Robin had sanctioned CN Group's sale to Newsquest. I didn't think he realised it would turn out like this.

That same month, the government-commissioned Cairncross Review into the future of UK journalism was published. It reported that more than three hundred local papers – a quarter of the total – had closed in the past decade. Another report said that the number of journalists on local papers had halved to about 6,500 since 2005.

The Cairncross Review mentioned an NUJ claim that in August 2018, Newsquest made ten redundancies in its Bradford office the day after its parent company Gannett announced that the changing value of the pound had given it a $13.2 million (£10.2 million) windfall and that shareholders would receive an $18.1 million (£14 million) dividend.

In the age of fake news, newspapers were struggling when they were needed more than ever. An estimated 58 per cent of the country had no local daily paper. Council and court proceedings were increasingly not reported. In 2017 the Grenfell Tower fire in the London borough of Kensington and Chelsea killed seventy-two people. A former journalist in the area, Grant Feller, told *Press Gazette* that residents' concerns about fire risks would have been picked up on if local journalism there hadn't been decimated during the previous decade. By the time of the fire, Kensington and Chelsea had one dedicated local paper. Its one reporter had to cover several boroughs.

Maintaining the quality of our papers became harder for those who remained. From being respected and essential, they were now ridiculed or ignored. Instead of contacting us with a story, people would post it to a Facebook group. It sometimes felt as if no one was reading our work any more. People often asked, 'Are you still at the paper?' This frustrated me. I took the decline personally.

In May 2019 Vanessa Sims, editor of our Barrow-in-Furness-based sister title the *Mail*, was appointed group editor for Newsquest Cumbria. Chris Story and the county's other editors would now report to her. Vanessa came up to Carlisle once a week. The office she used was next to the newsroom. I'd see her in there and wonder what she was planning. Trying to stay focused while waiting for the axe was draining.

Chris had advised the three remaining feature writers to tell anyone who enquired that we were writers, doing some news stories as well as features. This was true. And it was his attempt to protect our jobs. Feature writer: the job title that no longer dared speak its name. Long-form writing had become something to apologise for. Yes, sorry, there's a 1,200-word feature about an author. But don't worry – on the next page we've got a list of our Facebook readers' favourite nail bars.

Some features did well online. These were normally profiles of well-known people, and columns and colour pieces about topical issues. I wrote a column headlined 'Is cannabis legal now?' This was inspired by the growing frequency with which I smelled the drug around Carlisle: some days my walk home was more of a float. It received much more attention than better-written pieces that didn't capture readers' imaginations so easily.

Seeing one of my stories as the most popular on our website was great for my ego, if not my mental health. At weekends I'd log in as a staff member and spend hours on the homepage, clicking 'Refresh' every few minutes to see how many more hits my stories had received. Days passed in which I'd done little but monitor whether a feature or column had remained in our top ten.

By 2019 the website was getting more than 5 million page views a month. Those of us who were sceptical about our digital-first policy tried to discover, without success, how much money all these hits were making. We were reminded that the more hits our website received, the more companies would pay to advertise on it. I wondered if newspaper publishers around the world had secret sweatshops where people clicked on their stories 24/7.

Chris asked us to consider whether our least-viewed stories had been worth writing. I tried not to cover just crowd-pleasing subjects. But it was tempting to do that when we could all see how many hits, or how few, each story had.

A walk around his vast parish by the Bishop of Carlisle was an archetypal *Cumberland News* story. Online it died, apart from a few *Father Ted*-related Facebook comments. Did this mean we'd been wrong all those years to write that kind of story? Not if online was a different audience.

Anyone who'd only ever read our papers would have been bemused by our website. It included 'Promoted stories' with headlines such as 'Remember Meg Ryan? Where she lives now is sad' and 'Remember Emily from *Emmerdale*? Try not to smile when you see her now.' Clicking these sponsored links led to celebrity gossip sites.

Readers accused us of publishing our own clickbait. One Sunday, in September 2019, I looked at our site and saw two stories that each had the heading 'WEIRD UK NEWS': 'Man caught on film throwing chairs over mall balcony'; 'Grandmother who popped out to buy flowers woke up in hospital three days later unable to recognise ANY of her relatives.'

These national stories had been posted in an effort to attract more clicks. The mall – in Britain, I believe they're often known as 'shopping centres' – was in Bristol. The grandmother was in Carnforth, Lancashire. Readers' comments were not enthusiastic. One wrote about the grandmother story, 'I don't know how to say this. Could you . . . I don't know . . . look at a map? Please, for the benefit of us all? Carnforth is in Lancashire. This is Cumbria. What are you even doing?'

That comment delighted me. I told myself that chasing clicks with stories such as these was counterproductive: it wasn't worth the damage to our credibility. I told myself that people didn't want to read stuff like that. Often, though, they did. Our most-read stories around that time included 'Here's what is in the middle aisle at #Aldi and #Lidl this week'. And you know your career isn't going particularly well when all your stories are outstripped by 'Halloween fancy dress for dogs from Lidl'.

At one point the most-read stories were:

1. Thomas Cook fears going bust as travel firm may 'run out of money'.
2. The seven medical conditions you MUST tell the DVLA about.
3. Asteroid the size of a skyscraper due to pass by Earth.

The fact that people wanted to read these national stories more than any that we'd written wasn't great for my colleagues or me. Maybe readers clicked on some of them because they were incredulous that their local paper was now dishing up such stuff. I suspected that if it could be proved that people were clicking just to see what we'd been reduced to, Newsquest bosses wouldn't have cared. As long as they were clicking.

'WEIRD UK NEWS: Unlucky in love model reveals her worst Tinder dates.'

None of this bolstered the image of journalism as a noble profession. *Hold the Front Page* regularly reported on journalists being subjected to online abuse. The newspaper industry may be unique in giving the public a platform to insult its employees. Obnoxious comments attract clicks. And journalists are too busy to constantly monitor the flood of comments on their websites and social media channels.

Coventry Telegraph editor Keith Perry warned that 'truly appalling' abuse was becoming 'the new normal'. Amy Fenton, chief reporter at the *Mail*, said, 'I've been subjected to some of the most vile and vociferous abuse on social media solely for doing my job. I've been threatened, targeted, belittled and humiliated by mostly anonymous bullies who seem to relish the prospect of hurting and scaring me.'

One *Hold the Front Page* reader wrote, 'Negativity and abuse in general on an online platform are corrosive, they "permit" other people to take the same chances, they ruin perception of the brand . . . and they make it too unpleasant for moderate and normal people to comment.'

My column continued to attract abuse. I suggested that *Who Wants to Be a Millionaire?* contestants should be subject to a means test. If you're rich, you shouldn't be allowed on the show. I imagined the horror of watching über-toff Cabinet minister Jacob Rees-Mogg win a million quid and treat it as small change. This was clearly tongue in cheek. Well, it was clear to me. Facebook comments included:

'Absolute rubbish!'

'Oh shut up!!'

'What a load of utter drivel.'

Celebrities who are trolled can console themselves with the knowledge that their critics don't know the real them. At times I had no such solace. The 'utter drivel' comment was 'liked' on Facebook by a friend of a friend; someone I'd met.

These were toxic times, fuelled by Brexit. Conservative MP Rory Stewart's Penrith and the Border constituency was in our circulation area. He was often newsworthy, especially after being promoted to the Cabinet and standing to be party leader. During Brexit we ran frequent stories about Rory, all of which attracted bile on our Facebook page.

A *News & Star* leader column praised Rory's call for both sides in the Brexit debate to treat each other with respect. This message did not go down well with all our Facebook readers: 'i think it's time news and star apologies to its readers for this post and past posts, this is my last post on here i will be removing them from my facebook'.

People used to say they weren't going to buy our papers any more. Now they threatened to stop reading our work for free.

There was venom for Labour as well as for Rory the Tory. Someone wrote, 'Voting to give power to the EU, [Jeremy] Corbyn and his ilk should be a hanging offence.' That prompted me to write a column suggesting that a 2019 version of nicey-nicey 1970s game show *Mr and Mrs* would be very different.

'OK, Sandra. You disagree with Martin's views on Brexit. Do you, a) Decide not to discuss the issue because it gets you both hot under the collar; b) Have an in-depth discussion to understand each other's point of view; or c) Call him a traitor and say he should be hanged for treason?'

I hoped this might make people see the absurdity of abusing those who happened to have a different view about the UK's membership of the European Union. Instead the website comments became a slanging match. One reader, who wrote under the name Delbert Boomdocker, said of the column, 'What a load of tripe', followed by several paragraphs of anti-EU vitriol. Mr Boomdocker's response confirmed that people will take whatever they want from what they read, not what the writer might want them to.

The question of whether a keyboard warrior would express their views face to face remains one of the great twenty-first-century talking points. The theory is that they hide behind anonymity. No one ever approached me and said, 'Excuse me, do you get paid for writing this rubbish?'

I had a contact whom I'd interviewed several times and had given me numerous story ideas. In recent years he'd frequently criticised the *News & Star* on its Facebook page, referring to it as 'a failing rag'. One day I saw him in the street. 'I've read some of the things you've put on Facebook,' I said. 'You seem to have a bit of a downer on us.'

He looked embarrassed. He said that he was criticising falling standards in the hope of inspiring improvement. If that theory worked, the amount of inspiration our online readers gave us every day would have made us the best newspaper in the world.

The 'Not the News and Star' Twitter account continued its sniping. I'd interviewed Rory Stewart, and taken the pictures on my phone. In the middle of the main picture was Rory. So far so good. Around him were people: still fine. In the bottom-left corner was an arm. A disembodied arm, which appeared to have been left on a wall.

'Not the News and Star' brought this pic to the attention of its readers. One of them commented, 'Love that detached arm, left-hand bottom of the uncropped pic. Publishers such as Newsquest and Reach said there'd be no lessening of quality as photographers, sub-editors and experienced, truly local reporters were laid off in favour of callow (but cheap!) staff.' Indeed. And at my age it was flattering to be mistaken for callow.

There was plenty of material for anyone who wanted to highlight our decline. We ran weight-loss stories about people who'd lost two stone. There used to be an unofficial four-stone minimum before someone was deemed worthy of a mention. At this rate, another few years would see weight-loss stories about people who'd cut their fingernails and removed their jewellery.

Some journalists didn't seem to know what simple words meant: words such as 'admitted'.

'Although performing and acting take her round the country, she admitted, "I'm at home in the Lakes."'

That's not much of an admission, is it? She hasn't exactly revealed that she's a serial killer. A sub might have helped. The good ones were missed for their headline-writing and design skills.

The art of the headline was dying anyway with the rise of online journalism. Puns, or any kind of wordplay, are not encouraged in online headlines. We were told to build these around relevant place names and people's names to maximise the chance of anyone searching for those things to find them on our site.

As for design, in 2012 I'd written a column about Valentine's Day. The first few paragraphs described a February the fourteenth when I'd wanted to watch Carlisle United and my girlfriend had wanted us to have a meal instead. The page was beautifully constructed. The headline was 'Roses are red but I like the Blues. I'd rather watch them than stay in with you.' It was four lines, in alternate red and blue. There was a cut-out picture of me against a cut-out heart. The equivalent now would be a photo of any celebrity, and an online headline that included their name.

22

Nude Reporter Shares His Tip

I WROTE sympathetically about any group I reported on. That might have been difficult if the subject was sex offenders or Morris dancers. In general, though, being nice felt like respect for the fact that they'd allowed me into their world.

In 2018 Wigton Baths began hosting naked swimming sessions. I emailed the organisers, British Naturism, to ask if I could attend and interview some participants. They replied to say I'd be very welcome, as long as I got my cock out. That wasn't their exact phrase but it might as well have been.

I said that would be fine, thank you. The potential for a good feature overrode my embarrassment. I also saw British Naturism's stance as a challenge I wouldn't run from. This was an example of the suit of armour that being a journalist gave me, although I'd have to take that off before leaving the changing room.

Also – and I never expected to say this – I thought that taking my clothes off might help my career. Feature writing being regarded as a namby-pamby branch of journalism irritated me. Editors could look approvingly at the reporter who worked a twelve-hour shift when a big story broke or who approached someone with a violent reputation for a quote. But who was I? The feature writer who wrote about a community centre's new kitchen. Repeatedly.

A reporter friend often took the piss by asking, 'Are you working on any breaking features, mate?' I'd tell him that a press release about an art exhibition had just arrived so I'd be working through the night.

Sometimes I felt a need to go the extra mile. Such a lengthy unit of measurement wasn't really appropriate when it came to me being naked. But I knew it wouldn't do any harm to venture beyond the call of duty. This felt more important than ever under Newsquest. So swimming naked seemed a perfectly sensible thing to do, until I woke up on the big day.

I drove to Wigton. In the changing room I donned my birthday suit, and emerged with my largest towel draped over my shoulders. At the poolside I interviewed someone from British Naturism while feeling very self-conscious. To my surprise, this wasn't because I was naked. I felt self-conscious because I wasn't naked; not with the towel partially covering me. I took it off and felt much better for blending in with my fellow swimmers. Being the odd one out was scarier than being nude.

We had a freelance photographer there who I'd known for more than twenty years. He strolled in, fully clothed. There was none of the 'It's only fair that you should take your clothes off' business that I'd gone through. I resisted the temptation to point this out. The more clothes he wore the better as far as I was concerned. I'm sure he thought the same about me. We exchanged a look that said, 'This is a bit weird, eh?'

The biggest embarrassment came when he took my picture as I stood at the top of the steps with a strategically placed notebook. My anxiety prompted a super pout for the camera. But it was one of the most satisfying features I ever wrote. I was nervous before every colour piece: worrying about speaking to lots of people and getting good enough quotes. My anxiety had been heightened here by being naked. As was usually the case, though, everyone was friendly. And the quotes were good.

They've done naked taekwondo as well. What's the difference between that and regular taekwondo? Julie gave
me a pitying look. 'It's just the same, but without your
clothes on.'

As I left, the pool manager and the receptionist thanked me for
coming along. They also congratulated me on having the balls –
I'm paraphrasing – to take part. The swimmers had said the same.
I'd responded with faux modesty. Shucks – all in the line of duty/
no two days are the same in this job. I drove away. I'd done it! The
humiliating part of the day was just beginning.

Leaving the car park, the road went left and right. There were no
signs. Perhaps because my brain had been scrambled by nerves on
the drive in, I couldn't work out which way I'd arrived. Not that it
mattered. I'd checked the route the previous day. Either direction
would take me back to Carlisle.

I turned right. The narrow road climbed up a steep bend then
flattened out into a straight stretch. I soon saw that something
ahead was blocking my path. It was a gate. I got out to open it.
The road was so narrow that when I left the car I stumbled into
thorn bushes, swearing as they stabbed me.

The gate was locked. A chain was secured by a large padlock.
I examined it, rattled it, tried to work out what was going on.
However I looked at it, there was no way through. The road was
far too narrow to turn around. I'd have to reverse.

This was a problem. I've never been able to reverse in a straight
line. After just a few yards the car inevitably veers left or right.
And now I was faced with reversing along a dead straight stretch
of about three hundred yards with thorn bushes on one side and a
fence on the other. Why was this happening? I'd done the difficult

bit. I'd been photographed naked. Now I should be on my way home for a cup of tea.

After dragging myself back through the bushes and into the car, I began reversing . . . into the bushes. I tried again, and almost hit the fence. Most drivers would have made it back to the baths in about a minute. Gaining a few yards with each backwards-into-the-bushes-or-fence-then-forwards-again-to-straighten-the-wheels manoeuvre, it took me a quarter of an hour to reach the top of the hill. There was no way I could reverse down the steep, winding road. My reversing around a bend makes my reversing in a straight line look highly skilled.

At that point the road was just wide enough to attempt a three-point turn. Or in my case a thirty-point turn. As I began to manoeuvre, an elderly couple came walking up the hill. I got out to check that they had room to pass the car. 'Sorry,' I said. 'I'm just trying to turn around.'

'Why don't you open the gate?' said the man. 'That'll give you more room.'

Yes: on my right was a gate to a field. If I put the nose of the car in the entrance, there'd be plenty of room to reverse out then drive down the hill facing forward. 'I'll open it,' he said. I thanked him and began inching towards the gate. Then I thought, 'Why don't I just drive around the field and come out facing the right way?'

I entered the field and kept going. The couple looked alarmed. They were gesturing and shouting something. The car stalled. The world was suddenly quiet.

As I got out, my feet sank. It had been raining for days. The front wheels had churned up the grass and were stuck in a sea of mud. The man broke the silence. 'The grass is too wet,' he said. The words 'No shit' hovered on my lips.

I tried to reverse. The wheels spun helplessly. For the only time in my life outside the context of romantic disappointment, I put my head in my hands.

'I'm not sure what to suggest,' said the man. 'Well, we have to be going. Good luck.'

It was only about 3.30. But this was December. It would be dark soon. I thought about walking to the station and getting a train home. Then I imagined waking up next morning and remembering that I'd abandoned a car – a pool car belonging to my employer – in a field 12 miles away. I searched the glove box for details of a breakdown service, either for the car or for me, but found nothing.

My only plan now was to return to the baths. What a brilliant idea. Your car is stuck in a field. Who you gonna call? Nude swimmers.

I'd left there half an hour earlier thinking I'd made a good impression. Now I shuffled back in with my shoes and trousers caked in mud. My suit of armour remained in the changing room. This wasn't the journalist me. This was fearful, clueless me.

I mumbled to the receptionist, 'My car's stuck in a field.'

'Pardon?'

'My car . . . it's stuck in a field.'

The manager appeared. We went outside. I pointed to the car at the top of the hill.

'How did it get there?' she said.

I began by explaining that I'd gone the wrong way out of the car park, adding, 'I suppose that happens a lot?'

'No,' she said.

I told them that I'd tried to turn around in the field and got stuck. There were puzzled faces and murmurs of surprise but I was grateful for their lack of judgement. I didn't know what I expected them to do, but they began making phone calls.

'He's got his car stuck in a field.' Pause. 'I don't know – he just has.'

After several calls I was told that help was on its way. By now the baths had closed. But the manager and receptionist hung around until, about an hour after I'd returned, the receptionist's husband and son arrived in a van.

These were the kind of practical people I've always envied. They assessed the situation, with the help of another volunteer who'd turned up with a torch. A rope was tied between the van and the back of the car. The van eased forward. To my immense relief, the car came loose. The son then reversed it down the hill after I explained that I wasn't very good at doing that. God knows what they thought of me.

Here was the community spirit I'd been writing about for years. Three people rushing out in the dark to help some nutter they didn't know who'd driven into a sodden field.

That night I told a friend about my afternoon of nude swimming and off-road driving. 'You're like a pervert Frank Spencer,' he said.

Over the years there had been numerous examples of my driving struggles. I'd pull up outside someone's home and realise it would be difficult to leave. The worst were narrow driveways that plunged down from the road, so to get back out I'd have to reverse up a short, steep hill then turn sharply at the top without hitting a wall. As interviewees poured their hearts out, I'd be thinking, *If I pull the steering wheel hard down to the left when I reach the gatepost, I should be all right.*

The day after the Wigton Baths job, the photographer emailed me the pictures. The one of me standing on the steps caught my attention. My notebook was covering my midriff. But just visible underneath it was . . . what? Oh no: it was the tip of my penis! I replied immediately, pointing out that this could be seen. He emailed, 'It's not that big – it's your finger!' I looked again. My finger! I felt stupid for thinking it had been my dick.

The feature was published in the *Cumberland News* the following Friday. I'd had the sense to take the day off. A friend texted me early that morning. His text included the photograph on the steps. He'd drawn a circle around . . . whatever it was. His message read simply, 'What the fuck is that?'

Next day the story was published on our Facebook page with that picture. The first reader comment was 'Must add pigs in blankets to my Christmas food shopping list!!' In another photo I was swimming breaststroke. Someone wrote, 'Thankfully wasn't doing the backstroke when this picture was taken – put some shorts on ffs!'

I'd felt this feature deserved better than one of my workmanlike headlines. Super-sub Anthony Ferguson had moved to our magazines division. I emailed him for suggestions. He replied, 'Skin at the deep end'.

The reaction to the story was everything I craved. Amusement, respect, affectionate mockery. The subject matter ensured it was widely read, in the paper and online. I had more feedback for that feature than for anything I'd written in twenty-three years of journalism. For weeks, a day rarely passed without someone mentioning it. A postman shouted, 'You've got some clothes on today then?' Strangers in the street asked me about naked swimming. What was it like? Had I been embarrassed? And most frequently of all, was that my cock under my notebook?

Soon afterwards I wrote another piece that I was proud of: an interview with a former drug addict who'd been jailed for the attempted armed robbery of a shop. He was now clean, working, and keen to show addicts that they could turn their lives around. This feature was also well received. Online readers congratulated him and described his story as inspiring. The following week a reporter shouted across the newsroom. There was a call for me.

After writing something that I'd fretted over – a phrase in a profile, a fact I'd checked repeatedly but for whatever reason still had some doubt about – I dreaded the phone ringing. When complaints did arrive, they were almost always out of the blue. If I could have predicted them, I might not have written what they were complaining about.

A woman was on the line. She was the attempted robbery victim's wife. She was upset and asked how I'd thought she would feel when she opened the paper to see the man who'd brandished a gun at her husband. My voice started shaking in reply. I asked if I could call her back in a few minutes, and tried to work out what to say.

How had I thought she would feel? I'd tried to avoid thinking about that. It had crossed my mind that seeing the attacker in the *Cumberland News* might stir up painful memories. But no . . . they'd be pleased to see how much he'd changed and how sorry he was for what he'd done. They might even ask me to set up a meeting with him in which tears would be shed and apologies offered and accepted. What a story that would be.

Wishful thinking, I could see now. The empathy I'd felt for the robber had not extended to this family. Should I have warned them? Virtually every edition of every newspaper carries stories about criminals. Are papers supposed to contact all their victims before publication? On the other hand, I could see her point. Her husband had thought he was going to die. And I'd churned everything up again.

I rang the woman back, and tried to argue that this was a worth-
while story of redemption. 'You only care about selling papers,'
she said. It wasn't true. But I realised that I hadn't warned them
about the story because I was worried that they'd try to stop me
running it. I didn't only care about selling papers. I cared about
telling compelling stories. And I told myself that the end justified
the means.

23

Writers on the Storm

Every morning at 9.30 the editorial survivors had a meeting around one of the many empty desks. This meeting, to discuss the previous day's web figures and how we'd persuade people to click on our site today, was given the ironically cheerful name 'Breakfast Club'.

Avoiding meetings was near the top of my career ambitions. Most of my mental energy was expended on worrying about having to speak. There was little left to come up with anything creative. These meetings felt like being at school. Colleagues who trotted out a lengthy list of stories they were working on were patted on the head, as were those who'd generated plenty of hits the day before.

At other times we were collectively bollocked for failing to put enough of our stories online. Generally, Chris Story was remarkably calm. But days when our website fell far below its page-views target could prompt him to snap at us. It gave a hint of the pressure he was under. A few minutes later he'd take the mickey out of himself, often referring to a vein in his temple. 'That thing's going to pop one of these days.'

At Breakfast Club I reverted to being a teenager, sulkily staring into space and saying nothing unless responding to a question. I tried to dodge these meetings. When arranging an interview, the first thing I'd say was, 'Would nine-thirty be OK?' On the days I did attend, it was increasingly clear that features were an afterthought.

One morning in the summer of 2019, Breakfast Club came with a twist. Chris told us that Newsquest wanted organisations to supply the *News & Star* with stories and pictures. The organisations would write these stories to fit the shapes on certain pages. They were 'back of the book' stories: those published after the front few pages, which contained the best news stories. Back of the book was my territory. That was where features lived.

Google had given Newsquest a grant to develop technology for non-journalists to submit ready-for-publication content. Google, like Facebook with its funding of eighty trainee journalists, may have seen some commercial benefit in throwing the newspaper industry a few crumbs. Perhaps these companies wanted to prolong the life of papers so they could continue to capitalise on their work. Maybe it was a pre-emptive strike, to show the authorities in the event of any crackdown on their vast profits 'Look – we've given some cash to local papers.'

Newsquest appointed Simone O'Kane to oversee the ready-for-publication project in the north of England. It was being piloted in Cumbria. Simone said on *Hold the Front Page*, 'This is a fantastic way for publications to be achieving more in-depth and quality news reporting from professional journalists whilst working closely with community contributors that can submit the easy to generate content.'

Newsquest's editorial director Toby Granville described it as 'key to freeing up our valuable journalists' time to focus on the sort of high impact, in-depth reporting that remains central to the strength and trust of our brands.'

Some of us suspected that making it easy for the public to

submit content would free up Newsquest to get rid of journalists.

The *News & Star* already had 'Camera Club' – readers sent us scenic pictures and we filled a weekly spread with them – and 'School of the Week', in which a school sent in its own stories and pictures.

We were told to think about what other organisations we could contact to suggest sending us content. I imagined how that would have been received ten years earlier. Back then the newsroom had been packed with experienced, confident journalists. Now there was silence as we were asked to dig our own graves. I would never have had the balls to object, and now there was no one doing it on my behalf. Instead of protesting, I emailed Chris to suggest that charities would welcome publicity and had good stories to tell.

In early October we saw the result of all this: pages of features supplied for free from the outside world.

Every Monday there was now a page from one of the emergency services, a page from the Devil's Porridge First World War museum, two pages from a primary school, a page from a nursery, and a page from the University of Cumbria.

On Tuesdays less came from outside. But there were five pages of pictures from our archives, and a page from a bygone edition of the *News & Star*.

Wednesday: two pages from South Lakes Safari Zoo and Lake District Wildlife Park. And a nostalgia page, which had previously been used in one of our west Cumbrian sister papers.

Thursday: another recycled nostalgia page.

Friday: another recycled nostalgia page, two pages from Parkrun, a page from the local NHS, and half a page from the Citizens Advice Bureau.

'Camera Club' now filled a page every day. And there were Press Association features, such as celebrity interviews, with no local angle. Apart from sport, on some days the content written by our journalists ended at page thirteen in a forty-page paper.

We also started running a weekly page of obituaries. The text was the same as that in the original death notices, with the addition of pictures presumably supplied by the families. A colleague suggested that in future we could increase efficiency further by asking readers to write their own obituaries.

In September, BBC Scotland had screened a two-part documentary called *The Papers*. This examined life at Glasgow-based titles the *Herald*, the *Evening Times* and the *National*. They were all owned by Newsquest. In the past year the company had cut £1.4 million from editor-in-chief Donald Martin's budget. According to the documentary, ten years earlier the papers had about eight hundred staff. Now they had one hundred.

Another round of cuts was on the way. Donald said of Newsquest, 'The first thing they'll do is look at my staff list and say, "Well why do you need so many staff?" They don't believe we need any photographers. That you can get by with reader-generated pictures and your reporters going out with your mobile phone. Now, you're a national paper. So you're competing in a very tough marketplace. Quality is what we're all about.'

Later he added, 'Those cuts we've made have taken us right down to the bone. It's incredibly tough to produce quality newspapers if you don't have the resources.'

I admired Donald's openness, and was surprised that Newsquest had agreed to the documentary. Had the company known what would be revealed? Seeing the situation in Glasgow was like looking in a mirror.

***

On a Tuesday afternoon in October, Chris asked Mark Green and me into his office. Stephen Blease, the other feature writer, was on holiday. 'I've been asked to read you this statement,' said Chris. It was signed by Newsquest Cumbria's group editor Vanessa Sims and headed 'Restructure within the editorial departments, Cumbria'.

The statement said that the company continued to look at ways of reducing costs. When allocating resources, it considered how best to meet the requirements of its audiences. With this in mind, it was proposing to make the three Carlisle-based feature writers and a Kendal-based entertainment writer redundant. The company believed this would leave it more able to serve readers with 'the content they value'. The changes would result in one new role: a features and entertainment reporter covering the whole of Cumbria.

Chris said we could apply for the new job. We were told that, meanwhile, there'd be a consultation process to discuss ways of avoiding redundancy. As far as I knew, no one had ever emerged from a Newsquest consultation with their job. As it stood, we'd be leaving in five weeks.

Mark and I returned to our desks clutching envelopes containing the statement, a job description for the features and entertainment reporter role, and details of Newsquest vacancies around the UK. Chris had asked us not to tell anyone the news until he'd spoken to Stephen. As we sat down, another colleague looked across. Two feature writers are called into the editor's office and emerge carrying brown envelopes. She didn't need to be Sherlock Holmes to suspect that something was going on.

'Is everything all right?' she asked.

'Great,' I replied.

She wasn't convinced. Neither was I. I'd spent months wondering how I'd react to this. The answer was, more surprised than I'd expected. I'd been writing features that had been well received. I was well-known in the area. Now I realised that I'd thought I was immune. I'd thought I would escape the Newsquest features cull. They'd see me as too valuable.

I had a job at Carlisle Youth Zone in an hour. On the way there I thought about how much I'd miss this. Telling stories. Being part of things. Facing my fears. It was one of those jobs that involved wading out of my comfort zone: interviewing several people about a fundraising venture, then arranging dozens of children for a crap photo on my phone. Most of the adults there knew me from previous jobs or from seeing my picture in the papers over the years. I was Roger Lytollis from the *Cumberland News*. But not for much longer.

That night I managed two hours' sleep. My heart raced. It felt as if the ground was giving way. I was forty-nine, an age when I'd hoped my career would be approaching its peak. I didn't expect sympathy. This was just how life is now. We want to save money. We want, ideally, to pay nothing. That applies to news as much as anything. The price we do pay is poorer products, inferior conditions, redundancies.

None of the journalists I knew who'd been made redundant in the past few years had stayed in journalism. Those who moved into PR spoke of strange concepts such as being paid for overtime, and spending days catching up on work they'd fallen behind with rather than being expected to cram it in among the deadlines or do it at home. Many journalists chose to go into PR without having been made redundant. Some didn't seem to see a distinction between the two jobs. Those of us who defined ourselves as journalists had fewer options.

Others thrived in a range of different worlds. One former sub ran a coffee van. Another had a wine shop. A former photographer was now a gardener. A former reporter was a teacher. They all seemed happy. Sooner or later, someone's life would go the other way.

Newsquest issued a statement saying, 'Whilst these potential redundancies are regrettable, it means we can continue to invest in frontline reporters which are central to the continued success of our local news brands.' It had issued many similar statements in the previous few years.

Press Gazette ran the story with the headline 'Journalists warn fresh cuts by Newsquest in Cumbria will "damage" reputation of titles.' 'Not the News and Star' retweeted this, adding, 'The reputation of these titles was irrevocably damaged when they became pro-Tory rags.'

Some responses to BBC Cumbria's Twitter account were more sympathetic. 'Even if people aren't buying a hard copy, they may be reading on line, so the journalists are still needed.' Others were closer to what I'd grown used to. 'Crap newspapers anyhow no big loss if it sinks.'

In the newsroom, most colleagues said they were sorry. Some said they were angry. A few paused briefly before continuing past my desk: a serious case of redundancy. I wasn't annoyed with them. But it made me wish I'd spoken to all those who'd been in the same situation in previous years. Now I knew they'd have appreciated it.

Vanessa Sims and I had never spoken. I'd never talked with our regional MD David Coates either. Both spent one day a week in Carlisle. Even after the redundancy announcement, they barely acknowledged the features team. Our body odour must have been worse than we'd thought. Not that everyone who braved the subject of redundancy improved my mood. One colleague said, 'I'm not being funny, mate, but there's not much for you round here, is there?'

Within days of the announcement I spoke to the editors of the monthly magazines *Cumbria Life* and *Carlisle Living*. These had been part of CN Group and were bought by Newsquest along with the papers. I agreed to write a couple of features for them. Presuming I was made redundant, three or four pieces a month would be something to build on as I tried to establish a freelance career. The day after I'd arranged those features came news that the magazines' design staff were being made redundant. Their work would transfer to Newport in south Wales, 300 miles away.

The magazines were excellent. *Cumbria Life* was reigning Magazine of the Year at the Regional Press Awards. Newsquest published other magazines but they were inferior free publications, filled with adverts and syndicated editorial. There was no question of Newsquest improving its other titles to match *Cumbria Life*. The idea of investing in something and making it better seemed alien. This now applied to *Cumbria Life* itself. The company did the thing it knew best. It cut, and the spiral of decline familiar from Cumbria's newspapers looked like spreading to its magazines. My life raft was sinking before I'd clambered aboard.

In the past few years I'd seen people who were faced with redundancy drained of their enthusiasm. Now I understood how hard it is to sprint to the finish line when you know you've lost the race. My mind wandered. The business of arranging words into an order that flowed felt more complex than before.

I thought about applying for the new role of features and entertainment reporter. The only information was a generic job description that said the successful applicant should have 'a healthy interest in website analytics'. It could have been made for me.

***

The first meetings about the redundancy proposal came the Monday after Chris had broken the news. That morning, streets near the centre of Carlisle were cordoned off. A man was at the top of Dixon's Chimney, the city's tallest building, nearly as high as Big Ben. It was less than a hundred yards from our office.

The canteen window usually offered a perfect view of the chimney top. At first it was shrouded in mist after a sub-zero night. The mist cleared to reveal a body hanging upside down: a man with his shirt off. The shirt was caught halfway down the maintenance ladder that he'd climbed in the night. His foot seemed to be trapped between the ladder and the chimney. He wasn't moving. We assumed he was dead.

Chief reporter Phil Coleman was darting in and out, interviewing people and updating our website. As other reporters arrived they were dispatched to join him. A week earlier I'd have volunteered to write a colour piece. Now, I let them get on with it. Lurking among the reasons – I didn't feel part of things any more, my mind was all over the place – was a childish, *Screw them. They don't need feature writers: fine. Let's see how they do without me.* A week earlier, if I hadn't volunteered I'd have been sent out. But I was already on the margins.

They did pretty well without me. Although it's hard to mess up a story about a man hanging upside down from a massive chimney as a Coastguard helicopter hovers nearby. The risk of downdraft was too great for the helicopter to get close enough for a rescue. A huge cherry picker was summoned from Glasgow.

Meanwhile, the three feature writers went into separate meetings with Chris to discuss our futures. Chris had asked if we wanted to postpone them. That would have felt self-indulgent: look at the pain I'm pretending to feel at this tragedy. It was awful, clearly.

But it wasn't my tragedy. I could separate the man who was dead or dying outside from my own situation, as I'd had to with the families of Derrick Bird's victims and so many other desperately sad stories of illness and bereavement.

I'd been invited to come up with an alternative proposal to redundancy. There was no point in arguing to keep my current job. Whatever happened, that was about to disappear. I suggested becoming a dedicated *Cumberland News* writer. The *News & Star* was finished as far as features were concerned. But the *Cumberland News* still needed in-depth writing about local people and issues. I may as well have argued to be made Pope. It felt important, though, to offer a plausible suggestion.

When I left work that day, a mountain rescue team was about to bring the man down in the cherry picker. It was like a scene from a sci-fi film in which aliens are landing. Cars were parked on pavements. Crowds of people stared up, some through binoculars. Some sat in their cars, eating sandwiches.

We received letters and emails describing all this as distasteful. But curiosity is human nature. I'd made a living from asking strangers about their lives and others wanting to read it. I hadn't eaten sandwiches outside while staring up at Dixon's Chimney. I'd eaten mine in the canteen, while staring up at Dixon's Chimney. And how many people who condemned the vulgarity of gawping at the poor bloke had read about him online? Our stories about the incident had hundreds of thousands of hits.

The man was dead when they brought him down. Hypothermia and cerebral swelling, the inquest heard. We learned that he was Phil Longcake, a fifty-three-year-old grandfather. Two months later his family gave their first interview, to the *Guardian*. That summer Phil had told them that as a child he'd been sexually abused on a regular basis by someone who was still alive.

He then reported this to the police. The suspect was interviewed and released without charge. The police said there was insufficient evidence. Phil's son thought his dad planned to die on the chimney, to send a message to his alleged abuser.

Our photographer had taken jaw-dropping pictures of the body, some with the Coastguard helicopter alongside. None was ever published, in our papers or online. Not everyone took this approach. The *Guardian* revealed that Phil's daughter had reported 'several zoomed-in photographs to Facebook on the day but the social network refused to take them down, saying they did not breach its community guidelines'. After being contacted by the *Guardian*, Facebook removed the images and apologised to the family, 'for any upset caused'.

For weeks I couldn't look at the chimney without seeing Phil Longcake. Sometimes he still seems to be there.

24

'What's Your Name?'

M Y parents didn't have a phone until I was fourteen. Making calls used to entail going around the corner to the public toilet, which doubled as a phone box. There was the traditional struggle to insert coins when the pips sounded. If people were waiting I felt pressured to hurry, and self-conscious about being overheard.

That was also a problem at Mrs Cubby's house. Mrs Cubby was our next-door neighbour. She let us use her phone; a kindness we were careful not to abuse. When we did call a faraway friend or relative, the whole family – my parents, my brother and me – would assemble in her living room. I hated speaking on the phone in front of anyone. My phone voice was an embarrassed mumble, the embarrassment made worse by being told to speak up.

That didn't come easily. My dad was a fireman who often worked nights. He'd return in the morning and go to bed. At weekends and holidays I was asked to keep the noise down. Maybe that got into my head and became something unhealthy. 'Be quiet, please – your dad's trying to sleep' turned into 'Be quiet.' The older I got the quieter I grew, particularly with the turmoil of puberty.

I'm trying to work out why speaking on the phone felt so hard. It became a problem when I became a journalist. The newsroom was a busy place with plenty of chatter, except, it seemed, when I

229

was on the phone. At those times the room could feel like a library in a sponsored silence. My voice might be the only sound. The thought of everyone hearing me was mortifying.

I'd speak quietly, which was a problem if an interviewee was hard of hearing. And many people were in places that didn't lend themselves to quiet conversation. Every other interview seemed to be 'I'm on a train – I can't hear you!' or 'You're going to have to speak up – I'm in a wind tunnel!'

My unease about speaking, and about just being me, was deep-rooted. Growing up, I felt odd. Maybe most children do. My name made it worse. I was embarrassed about having an unusual one in a world of Marks and Johns. By the time I was fifteen that discomfort had subsided. Then, watching *Blackadder* one night, I heard the word 'rogering' for the first time. Its meaning was all too clear. Brilliant – just what a painfully self-conscious teenager needs to enhance their life.

For a few years, rogering was part of sitcom and panel show vocabulary. I winced every time I heard it. Some people laughed when I said my name. That made a pathetically deep impression. I laughed along. But when people mocked my name, it felt as if they were mocking who I was. During a summer job in a factory I told everyone my name was Paul.

When I became a journalist, I'd sometimes stammer when saying my name. At first this was only ever on the phone. Then it began happening in person. Maybe it was a form of self-sabotage, born from the feeling that I didn't deserve to have it easy. *OK, dickhead. You can interview. You can write. But here's where you fall down – you can't say your name.*

People introduced themselves. I'd just say 'Hello.' I dreaded hearing, 'I didn't catch your name.' At that point I'd blurt it out and hope for the best. I'm not sure how much people noticed this struggle, which took place mostly in my mind.

Things came to a head the night I was cut out of a car for the feature about firefighters which I mentioned earlier. When the roof was ripped off, one of them leaned over me and asked my name. I was sure I'd stumble over it. So I stayed silent, taking deep breaths and preparing my attempt.

'What's your name?'

He probably thought I was in the role of a crash victim, unable to speak. At some point I was going to have to tell him. But my brain and mouth had become disconnected.

'WHAT'S YOUR NAME?'

I still didn't reply. I knew people were watching on Facebook. Maybe they'd be able to hear the firefighter shouting to me, and me not saying anything and, at some point, me stammering. After another deep breath, I said my name. Relief flooded in . . . then the worry that next time would be even worse.

This incident sparked an idea that spared me that trauma on future jobs. As soon as I met someone, I'd hand them my business card as a pre-emptive strike. You want to know my name? There it is in black and white.

In my late teens and early twenties I'd seen therapists about the depression that plagued me. Then journalism gave me a sense of purpose and a belief that I was good at something. But anxiety could quickly return. Just before talking to a celebrity or taking part in an activity for a colour piece, I'd be desperate for it to be over. On the way to jobs, a nervous sweat occasionally erupted. This would be under control by the time I arrived. Usually.

I interviewed the CEO of advertising agency Saatchi & Saatchi, who had a home in the Lake District. It was a hot day. I was late after getting lost. I was stressed about not being on time, and because this was a feature I'd been planning for weeks and which had the potential to be really good, if I could pull myself together. As the interview began, sweat pooled in my hair and poured down my face. The CEO offered me some paper towels and asked if I was OK. I was fine – doesn't everyone start raining now and then?

I never told anyone about this kind of anxiety, or heard anyone discuss similar problems. Journalism retained an old-school approach to mental health. It was a tough job and even the women had to man up. When a colleague heard anyone complain that journalism was stressful in some way, he'd say, 'We're not digging for coal,' or 'We're not lion taming.'

I knew he was right, but the anxieties consisted of more than nerves before a job. There was the tight feeling in my stomach as deadlines rushed towards me. The guilt over stories I hadn't written or people I hadn't interviewed through lack of time. Some stories remained on my 'to do' list for months. Some never left it.

The urge to do stories justice manifested itself in countless hours of unpaid overtime at home. Researching topics and interviewees. Wondering what to ask. Rehearsing questions in my head or out loud. Waking in the early hours to scrawl down ideas. And, most of all, writing. Going through each mass of background notes and quotes again and again to find what was buried.

Even if I wrote something good, it could always have been better. I could have asked more searching questions and brought my subject to more vivid life. Then it was back to square one and the hunt for new stories. Having used up so much energy in the line of duty, friends, family and partners were neglected. All for the sake of telling strangers' stories. How could I hope to understand them when I didn't understand myself?

25

Goodbye

I'D been shortlisted again in the North West Media Awards. Even colleagues who enjoyed taking the piss out of my defeats were rooting for me. 'Imagine if you won, when they're about to make you redundant?' Funnily enough, I had imagined that. But normal service resumed. I didn't win.

Next day was my interview for the features and entertainment reporter job, which I still knew very little about. I feared it would be an attempt to cram the four jobs that were being made redundant into one. But I didn't want to leave, and asked for an interview in case it turned out to be OK. Mark Green had his interview first. When he returned, I asked, 'What does the job involve?'

'Everything,' he said.

Vanessa Sims explained that it involved responsibility for six weekend supplements across Cumbria: those of the *Cumberland News*, the *News & Star*, and the Newsquest papers in Workington, Whitehaven, Kendal and Barrow. Many journalists cover a particular patch, such as a town or part of a city. This patch was the third-biggest county in England.

Some of those weekend supplements were hefty publications. The features and entertainment reporter would have to write much of their content and source the rest from the Press Association and various contributors. They'd have to find pictures for these stories, sub the stories, put them on the papers' numerous websites and social media channels, and chase up contributors if they hadn't sent their copy. They'd also be writing for the main sections of the papers as well as the supplements. I tried to look interested, while thinking that I'd rather chew my toenails off than take the job.

When Mark went for his interview, I noted how long he was away from his desk: twenty-eight minutes. *That's not long*, I thought. *How can a job interview take less than half an hour?* I was back in twenty-six minutes. 'I see what you mean,' I said.

Early next morning, a Saturday, I emailed Vanessa to thank her for the interview and to say I didn't want the job. I wasn't taking the risk of being offered it, in case that meant I'd lose the chance to leave with a redundancy payment: albeit on terms that had, of course, been reduced by Newsquest to the statutory minimum. I told her I was passionate about feature writing and it sounded as if this job wouldn't allow enough time for it. That was true. It also sounded as if it wouldn't allow enough time to fart.

On Monday I told Mark about my email. He said that he'd sent a similar one. Neither of the other two redundancy-threatened writers had applied for the job. So now we waited to leave.

That month – November – Newsquest's parent company Gannett was bought by another American company, New Media Investment Group. The companies agreed to merge under the Gannett name. The new firm became the largest newspaper business in the US. It said it would aim to cut $275 million to $300 million in costs each year. That seemed an incredible amount to save as a one-off. But every year? If anyone could, Gannett could.

New Media's CEO Michael Reed said that only about 25 per cent of the combined company's revenue came from digital. The struggle to make all those clicks pay wasn't confined to the UK.

We were sent an email relating mainly to the American part of the business. This said the merger would lead to redundancies. It also said the new company was more committed than ever to local news and proud of its journalists. 'If anything,' it added, 'we expect you will see an improvement in quality.'

Newsquest made most of its savings at the end of each year. The company's pre-Christmas cull was as much a part of the festive season as Slade and indigestion. I'd noticed this annual bloodletting even before Newsquest bought CN Group. *Hold the Front Page* had reported job cuts around the country every November and December.

That November was particularly brutal. In Glasgow more cuts were coming to the *Herald*. Newsquest invited applications for voluntary redundancy, saying that unless enough people came forward by the following week, it would have little alternative but to look at compulsory redundancies.

A Newsquest spokesperson told *Hold the Front Page*, 'Whilst these potential redundancies are regrettable, it means we can continue to invest in quality journalism for many years to come.'

The company was renowned for investing in quality journalism by getting rid of journalists. The *Guardian* reported that in 2009 the Glasgow papers had about two hundred and forty journalists, and that Newsquest was now planning to leave the *Herald* with six reporters.

The *Herald* accepted nine applications for voluntary redundancy. Newsquest's Christmas cuts kept coming. Five journalists' jobs were set to be made redundant at three south-coast dailies, as were three jobs in Lancashire. The two remaining photographers at the company's north- and mid-Wales titles were going, along with those papers' advertisement design teams. A feature writer and a deputy sports editor in Swindon. A photographer in Berkshire. A content manager and a sports editor in Darlington. A sports journalist in Essex. A production editor in Sutton.

A Newsquest spokesperson told *Hold the Front Page*, 'Whilst these potential redundancies are regrettable, it means we can continue to invest in quality journalism for many years to come.'

There were further departures in Cumbria. The position of editor at the *Cumberland News* and *News & Star* was being made redundant. Chris Story would be leaving the following week. That was devastating for our papers, and for morale. But Chris had wanted out. We were pleased he was escaping his punishing hours, the stress of being involved in colleagues' redundancies and the frustration of trying to maintain quality despite impossible odds.

The positions of editor at the Kendal-based *Westmorland Gazette* and associate editor at the *Whitehaven News* and the Workington-based *Times & Star* were also made redundant. Vanessa would be in charge of all Newsquest's papers across Cumbria, and all its magazines.

Around the country Newsquest laid off fourteen IT staff. You could have written an expanded Newsquest version of 'The Twelve Days of Christmas', starting at fourteen for 'IT technicians clearing their desks'. They included the only one left in Carlisle, who'd been covering the whole of Cumbria. The argument that she wasn't needed was undermined on her last day. We received an email saying that her leaving presentation had been cancelled. She'd been called to Barrow, nearly two hours away, to fix a problem.

Meanwhile, Newsquest's CEO Henry Faure Walker – he of the £500,000-plus salary – called on taxpayers to help fund the regional press. He said the government 'should support local journalism . . . for the next three to five years . . . Local journalism is a huge public good ... government needs to get out of the slow lane and be bold – otherwise our local communities ... will deteriorate just at a time when we as a nation need them most.'

I'd have felt more sympathy if Newsquest wasn't making enormous profits. And it occurred to me that my situation may have been caused by an outside body giving money to the newspaper industry. After all, Google had given Newsquest a grant to make it easy for non-journalists to provide news and features free of charge. Within days of that happening, Newsquest had proposed making my fellow feature writers and me redundant.

Things had gone quiet on that front, other than my suggestion of becoming a dedicated *Cumberland News* writer being rejected. We were due to leave the following week but that hadn't been confirmed. One night, Chris rang to tell me that we were being sent an email. Newsquest had moved the goalposts.

The initial redundancy statement had said we were invited to apply for the new role. Now we were told that one of us would have to do it. We'd each undertake a 'skills assessment exercise'. Its criteria included attendance, performance and disciplinary record. The 'winner' would be rewarded with the job that none of us wanted.

We contacted the NUJ, which told Newsquest it couldn't force any of us into a job that was so different from the ones we'd been doing. Feature writing would be a sideline to the main role of filling and subbing six supplements a week. A union rep came up from Manchester and put our case: we are feature writers. If that job isn't required any more, make us redundant and find someone who wants to do the new job.

The rep agreed with us that this was an unusual situation: a union arguing that its members should be made redundant. But she also agreed that the new job would have a ridiculous workload. I imagined being pushed into it, and walking out soon after because it was unbearable.

Early next week we received an email saying that the proposal to make us redundant would probably go ahead. On Thursday morning Chris called the three of us into his office, one at a time. We'd be leaving tomorrow. He thanked me for my years at CN, as we still referred to it. I thanked him. He was leaving tomorrow as well. One of the other editors whose jobs were disappearing would take the features and entertainment reporter role, to my immense relief. I hoped they'd cope with it better than I would have.

The past few weeks had brought plenty of digital delights. Instead of despairing, I used this to tell myself it was the right time to go.

Stories on the *News & Star*'s Twitter account included 'McMuffin fans rejoice: McDonald's are now doing breakfast until 11 a.m. in all restaurants across the country'.

I saw an advert for Newsquest's new Central Digital Content team. It asked for 'Deft skill at creating, rewriting and versioning snappy content with personality'. I had never knowingly versioned anything.

Toby Granville, the company's editorial director, sent an email saying that November's website traffic was up. 'You're all knocking it out of the park!' he wrote. I was barely knocking it as far as the swings.

Chris told us that web targets were likely to become much higher. Perhaps a colleague had this in mind while writing about a play being staged in the Lake District; a satire concerning Kim Kardashian. They put the story on our website with the headline 'Kardashians in Cumbria'. There wasn't even one Kardashian in Cumbria, which is their loss.

Despite its inaccuracy, the headline remained unchanged

because this became the most-read story of the day. With an accurate headline, that kind of story would have been nowhere near our top ten. This one was viewed thousands of times. All the comments accusing us of being 'clickbait wankers' were considered a price worth paying.

On some other newspaper websites I'd noticed a trend for news stories to get to the heart of the matter gradually. Reporters were traditionally taught to put the most important facts first. Now many intros only hinted at what was to come before the essence of the story was revealed several paragraphs later. I'd thought this was just poor writing. A former colleague suggested it was so publishers could tell advertisers that readers were scrolling further down each page, and were therefore exposed to more adverts.

***

On my last day, I logged into the various editorial systems. One of them had a tick box marked 'Remember me'. I'd never really noticed it before. For the first time since this had started, I welled up. Would anyone remember me?

Five of us were leaving: the three feature writers, Chris and a sports reporter. Only the sports reporter would be replaced, by a trainee.

There were no subs left to create any leaving pages. The editorial department that day comprised nearly as many leavers as remainers. Everyone else in the building trooped into the newsroom for a hastily arranged presentation. There were still far fewer bodies than there would have been in just editorial a few years earlier. In 2008: sixty-four editorial staff. Now fifteen would be left, most of them trainees.

Chris gave speeches about the other four departees before his deputy paid tribute to him. Then I finished clearing my desk, a process that had begun a couple of days earlier.

There were piles of books whose authors I'd interviewed.

Letters so old that the sticky bits of the envelopes had yellowed. Some were complimentary; some from charities saying they'd had a surge in support after something I'd written. It was good to feel I'd made a difference.

Notebooks: pages of scribble, which I hoped had translated into something meaningful for readers.

Photographs of the field in Wigton where, a year earlier, I'd sunk a car in mud. The following week our photographer had taken some pictures there and put them on my desk.

Old newspaper cuttings. After *24* crashed and burned, editor Dave Helliwell had wanted my column to continue, in the *News & Star*. On its first day there, the front page included my picture and the words 'Cumbria's funniest columnist'. A copy had been left on my desk with 'What the fuck?' scrawled across the top, 'funniest' changed to 'fanniest', and 'COCK' written on my forehead.

A *News & Star* from December 1999, twenty years ago almost to the day. Page two had the pictures and contact details of twenty journalists. I was one of just two still there. Phil Coleman would be the last man standing.

Some of the stories in that paper felt so recent. Time was always tricking me, as when searching our digital archive for a story I'd written three or four years ago, only to find it had been ten years.

At midday – precisely – I headed for the canteen with Phil, waving my lunchbox to cheers from those who'd noticed my daily routine. Back in the newsroom there were a couple of stories to finish. I could have done them in less than an hour. But I didn't want the end to come.

That afternoon Robin Burgess's widow rang each of the feature writers. She asked how I was. 'You've just got to get on with it,' I said, while having no idea how to do that. The past few months had taught her plenty about facing bigger tests.

The last thing I wrote was a *News & Star* leader column. I don't recall what it was about. It probably urged the Cumbrian public to shop locally this Christmas or demanded Prime Ministerial intervention over a blocked drain.

Mark Green said goodbye. The feature writers had become closer in the past couple of years, sharing a gallows humour as we felt the walls closing in. We shook hands and I tried not to cry. Then I wandered deserted corridors, wondering where twenty-four years had gone. The pool table was still in the canteen, hardly used for the past decade. I remembered the people I'd played against. Tony Greenbank came to mind. He was a veteran even on my first day in the newsroom, when he was the only one to look up from his screen and smile at me.

There used to be a *Cumberland News* feature called 'Working Life'. Someone would fill in a questionnaire about their job. The questions included 'Describe a typical day'. Everyone's answer could be guaranteed to include one of these three phrases: 'There's no such thing as a typical day' / 'Every day is different' / 'No two days are the same.' They might have worked on a production line, but there was no such thing as a typical day.

In the past few weeks I'd thought about how varied my job was. Occasionally someone I interviewed would say, 'Your job must be really interesting.' I'd reply on autopilot. The phrase I always used was 'You get a glimpse into lots of different worlds.' And it was true. Journalism had given me access to the famous and the powerful, to ordinary people with extraordinary stories. It had taken me to places I would never have known. It had given me everything. Satisfaction, confidence, partners, friends, a living, a life. I'd always loved the job. For all its stresses, it lifted me more than it weighed me down.

Back at my desk, I looked around for the last time. I'd seen countless others in this situation and wondered what they were thinking and feeling. I'd been here myself when leaving for Edinburgh. But maybe then I'd sensed I'd be back. This really was the end. Not blinking in case it dislodged the tears, I shook hands with Chris and waved goodbye to the almost deserted newsroom.

Clutching two bin bags stuffed with books and notebooks, I walked down the steps at the front of the building and remembered sitting on them one hot afternoon in the summer of 1995, waiting for a photographer to give me a lift to a job. Half my life ago. Everything still to come.

Epilogue

THERE had been little time to arrange a leaving do. Fortunately that night coincided with the editorial Christmas party. There were no dubious party games. The evening ended in handshakes and embraces.

For the next few weeks I kept visiting the *News & Star* website to see which stories were most read and to look at readers' comments. That was my life and I didn't have another yet. My last column was about the repeated calls to make James Bond a more sensitive character. Facebook comments included 'It's a film, you spaz, get ova ya self.' Someone else wrote 'What are you going on about now.' In their Facebook profile they described themselves as having 'a caring nature'.

Ahead of the December 2019 general election, around the UK political parties produced campaign literature in the style of newspapers. Toby Granville wasn't happy about this. The Liberal Democrats had created something they called the *Mid Hampshire Gazette*. Toby tweeted, 'This is outrageous, passing yourselves off as the Gazette newspaper in same area as our *Basingstoke Gazette*. If this isn't pulled I'll advise all Newsquest editors not to publish any campaign news for your party in build-up to #GE2019.'

Newsquest also made an official complaint to the Lib Dems, sending a copy of its letter to the Electoral Commission. The letter called on the party to destroy any remaining copies of its publication and issue a public apology. It claimed that the *Mid Hampshire Gazette* 'flagrantly mimics for partisan political purposes the name, style, layout and content of an independent local newspaper . . . Your publication therefore casts damaging and false imputations on Newsquest Media Group's editorial independence and seriously undermines the relationship of trust and confidence between readers and local newspapers generally.'

The day before the election, the *News & Star* was published in a Brexit Party wraparound. Identical in name and style to a normal *News & Star*, the front page had the headline 'Without the Brexit Party there can be no real Brexit'.

By that stage the *News & Star*'s average daily sale was fewer than 6,000: down by around 80 per cent since 2005 when the steep decline had begun. The *Cumberland News*'s sale was down by about 70 per cent in the same period. The *Edinburgh Evening News* had lost more than 80 per cent of its sale since my stint there in 2001.

National papers had diminished nearly as much as locals. *Today* closed in 1995, a few months after my column appeared there, because its 500,000 circulation was considered too low by its owners. By 2019 just two daily papers – the *Sun* and the *Daily Mail* – were selling as many as 500,000. In the preceding decade, national newspaper circulations had fallen by an average of 55 per cent. But some media organisations were thriving. In 2020 a report by the Competition and Markets Authority found that Facebook and Google were taking 80 per cent of the UK's digital advertising spend.

COVID-19 emerged in China in December 2019, and by March had travelled the world. Its devastation extended to already struggling newspapers. Many businesses stopped advertising. Lockdowns were not conducive to selling papers. Newsquest was the first newspaper group to put staff on furlough leave, which saw the government pay 80 per cent of their salaries. Those furloughed included the company's last photographer in Cumbria. Staff who remained had 15 per cent of any wage over £18,000 cut.

A *Times* leader column described local papers' struggles, saying, 'Rarely has access to reliable news been more important in saving lives.' *Times* leader writer Martha Gill tweeted, 'Here's our leader on the local press which is now in serious trouble. National papers aren't doing well either. You may not like all of them, but you'd miss them if they went.' Responses included:

Actually I wouldn't. I don't trust a single word I read in any paper nowadays.

Probably not. You are a disease.

Many journalists were suffering even worse abuse. In February 2020 a man was jailed after commenting on the *Mail*'s Facebook page that Cumbria-based reporter Amy Fenton 'needs raping'. Three months after that, Amy fled her home when police told her they believed there was a risk to her life. She'd been threatened after writing a court report. She told the *Guardian* that she'd wanted to be a journalist since she was a child. 'I love that we can champion people's causes and fight for decency and morality and fairness, even though there is never anyone fighting for us.'

In July, Amy pleaded guilty at Workington Magistrates Court to possession of cocaine and to driving while under its influence. She was fined and banned from driving for a year. Several weeks later she left the *Mail*. I thought about removing all reference to her from this book. But that would have felt like a cover-up. And while the messenger might be viewed as tarnished, the message about journalists being unappreciated and abused remains valid.

In May people around the world had protested against the killing of George Floyd: a black man who died in Minneapolis after a white police officer kneeled on his neck for nearly nine minutes. In the US more than a hundred journalists were attacked, by protestors and by police. President Trump, for whom journalists were 'the enemy of the people', had tweeted, 'The Lamestream Media is doing everything within their power to foment hatred and anarchy . . . they are FAKE NEWS and truly bad people with a sick agenda.'

A study by the UK's communications regulator Ofcom found that 80 per cent of internet-using adults had seen false or misleading information about coronavirus. Around the country, forty phone masts were vandalised after online claims that 5G wireless technology was to blame for the virus.

The newspaper industry launched a Twitter campaign: #buy apaper. National and local journalists used this to highlight the problems facing journalism, and the importance of accurate information amid a swamp of fake news. The replies to their tweets included images of newspapers being burned, references to newspapers being useful during toilet-paper shortages, and thousands of other derogatory comments. The power of answering back en masse, taking control from what they regarded as the Establishment, was irresistible to many.

> Haven't bought a newspaper for years – too many lies, too much right wing propaganda. The number of decent journalists in this country can be counted on one hand.

> The #buyapaper tag is f*cking hilarious. The British media is truly awful. I hope they all go bust.

That fate would have prevented stories such as the *Sunday Times*'s meticulous report into the government's arguably lax pandemic planning; the *Scottish Sun* revealing that Scotland's chief medical officer made two trips to her second home during the first lockdown; the *Daily Telegraph* reporting that the scientist whose advice led to the lockdown was visited during it by his married lover. The *Guardian* and the *Daily Mirror* broke the news that Dominic Cummings, Prime Minister Boris Johnson's chief adviser, had driven his family from London to Durham during lockdown, while his wife had Covid.

Some people criticised the media for grilling the government during such a testing time. Several journalists made the point that if China had a free press to question its leaders and report allegations, its people would have been told about Covid much earlier, potentially halting its spread before it became a pandemic.

The UK's press was under increasing threat. The NUJ was engaged in more than four thousand redundancy consultations, most of them linked to the impact of coronavirus. In June, Newsquest announced more redundancies nationwide. The NUJ reported that at least thirty-eight editorial jobs were going.

In Cumbria the vanishing jobs included the features and entertainment reporter role that I'd fought against being pushed into six months earlier. The Google-funded community contributors' project, which I felt had contributed to mine and several other jobs disappearing, was shortlisted in the Innovation and Initiative category at the Regional Press Awards.

Reach made 580 redundancies as it struggled with plunging revenue. The BBC cut more than 1,100 jobs in regional and national TV and radio. Some cuts were the result of a coronavirus-related funding shortfall. Others were part of an existing savings drive.

Covid prompted the *Guardian* to axe 180 jobs. The *Evening Standard* and DMG Media – publisher of the *Daily Mail*, *Metro* and *i* – each cut around a hundred. Newsquest Cumbria's last photographer came back from furlough, was furloughed again, and made redundant a few days later.

By the time you read this, many more journalists, sales staff and other media workers are likely to have lost their jobs at local and national level.

Newsquest and JPI Media were among the publishers that responded to the crisis by introducing some form of subscription or paywall for their websites: arguably twenty years too late.

Some of those who had remained at Newsquest Cumbria after my departure left because they couldn't stand what their job had become. Former BBC journalist Waseem Zakir had invented the word 'churnalism'. It describes the relentless process of turning press releases, news agency copy and social media posts into stories. This was how thousands of office-bound reporters now spent their days.

From January 2020 Newsquest Cumbria journalists were emailed a weekly league table, ranking them by how many page views their stories had received. It was tied to a nationwide bonus scheme that often rewarded those who sourced the most effective clickbait, rather than those who produced the best journalism.

By the end of 2020, Newsquest's six newspapers in Cumbria had no photographers, no feature writers, no sub-editors and one sports journalist. Most of the remaining reporters were trainees or had recently qualified.

On my penultimate day at Newsquest, I'd bought a six-month subscription to the *Cumberland News*. I loved that paper. But as the weeks went by, I realised I was torn. Cumbria needed a strong newspaper to inform and entertain, to hold the powerful to account. People I'd worked with for years and those learning their trade were doing their best in more challenging circumstances than ever.

And part of me was pleased to see the paper littered with mistakes, missing out on stories, increasingly filled with press releases and Press Association features. Look how it's gone downhill since I left. And look at me, bitter that life was continuing without me.

I'd been dumped. Get over it. Move on.

Afterword

THE hardback edition of this book was published in 2021. Many readers were journalists and ex-journalists who felt that someone was telling their story. Maybe not the naked swimming and the masturbating stripper, but the decline of the industry. The book sparked debate about the future of local newspapers. *Press Gazette* editor, Dominic Ponsford, wrote a comment piece. The replies included, 'Journalists today are utter scum and millions cheer when job cuts and paper closures are announced. Get over yourselves you absolute losers.'

Much else in local journalism also seemed like more of the same. The high staff turnover at my former papers continued. I've mentioned that when I was made redundant at the end of 2019, fifteen people remained in Carlisle's editorial department. By 2022, twelve of them had left. Any replacements were generally much less experienced.

After the Covid-era jobs cull, the big newspaper groups recruited digital journalists. Around the country, dozens of online-only titles launched. Many closed within a couple of years as the struggle to make money online continued. During 2023, Reach announced more than 800 redundancies. That year, print still accounted for 75 per cent of the company's revenue.

The shift to working from home that began during lockdown continued. Most regional publishers closed offices. Future generations of journalists may never know the collaboration and camaraderie that improved stories and helped to make the job enjoyable. To its credit, Newsquest tended to keep offices open, albeit often moving to smaller premises. CN Group's head office, which housed my newsroom, opened in 1972 and closed in 2022. It had become far too big for the few remaining staff. Head office is now a much smaller building across the car park. The former HQ is empty with many of its windows boarded up.

This isn't a cheery assessment of the state of local papers. They're swimming against the tide more than ever with so many sources of information to compete with, not all of them reliable. TikTok is now a bigger source of news for young people than newspapers. The main thing local papers have going for them is their staff. Increasingly overworked, underpaid and underappreciated, they continue to work daily miracles.

Since my redundancy, I've been a freelance journalist and author. Little, Brown commissioned me to write a travelogue about Britain's statues. There were launch events for that book and this one. No one died. Bearing in mind the horrors I'd imagined if I ever tried public speaking, that's enough to qualify them as a success.

I'm hoping to write more books. But I still think of myself as a journalist.

September 2024

Acknowledgements

THANKS are due to my former colleagues at CN Group/ Newsquest Cumbria and the *Edinburgh Evening News* for their help and entertainment value during the often stressful business of producing newspapers and bunging stuff on websites.

Particular thanks to Jon Colman, who unknowingly inspired me to work harder following his arrival at CN, through his annoying habit of being much better than me.

Also, Anthony Ferguson and the other sub-editors who enhanced my work; Alison Sisson and Elaine Little, for pretty much everything; and Pam McClounie and Nick Griffiths, for keeping me insane.

The National Union of Journalists was always in our corner during negotiations about pay and conditions. Jane Kennedy was especially supportive during my final weeks at Newsquest Cumbria.

Lou Laval sparked the idea for this book by giving me *This is Going to Hurt* – Adam Kay's brilliant memoir of his years as a junior doctor – and her encouragement spurred me on.

Tom Easterby's forensic analysis of my manuscript was very helpful.

Peter Hill and Richard Eccles made insightful suggestions and helped me to unearth half-buried memories from our years at CN.

With his author photo Stuart Walker managed to minimise my pout, for which we should all be thankful.

Mike Craven's evil genius was recognised when *The Puppet*

Show won the 2019 Crime Writers' Association Gold Dagger award for best crime novel of the year. I'm extremely grateful for Mike's assistance and advice about the publishing world.

Likewise, David Headley at DHH Literary Agency.

Hold the Front Page's comprehensive coverage of the local press was crucial in providing nationwide examples of the state of the industry: holdthefrontpage.co.uk

The same applies to *Press Gazette*'s coverage of the wider journalism world: pressgazette.co.uk

O_2 sponsored the North West Media Awards for most of my defeats and my sole victory. Thanks to them, and to the event's organisers Liz and Mark Rossiter of Rossiter Media.

'Panic as man burns crumpets' is a legendary bill from Surrey paper the *Staines News*, written by Oliver Florence. The paper reported that the panicking man called the fire brigade and was treated for smoke inhalation. The crumpets' condition is not known.

At Little, Brown: Duncan Proudfoot, publishing director of the Robinson imprint, was enthusiastic about this book from the outset. His guidance was invaluable.

Editor Rebecca Sheppard's plate-spinning skills and patience were very much appreciated.

Copy editor Howard Watson's diligence greatly enhanced my manuscript.

Sophie Harris and Steve Leard created the perfect face for this book with the concept and design of its amazing cover.

Thanks also to Beth Wright, Amanda Keats, Megan Phillips, Tabatha Aldred, Allison Garvey, Linda Silverman, John Fairweather and Riana Dixon.

My parents, Olga and Robert, have been hugely supportive throughout my career, and good-humoured whenever I've written about them.

Special thanks to Andrea, my beautiful partner, for her love and kindness.

Thank you to the thousands of people I've interviewed for sharing their stories.

And finally, to the readers, without whom I'd be shouting in an empty room. Thinking about what my life would have been like without journalism, that's probably more than a metaphor.

Index

advertising revenue 118, 119, 159, 183

alcohol-related features 85–9

Allen, Dave 75

apprentice journalists 177, 178, 181

Argus 158

Ault, Richard 136, 137

awards 131–7, 184, 233

battle re-enactments 63–4

Baty, Elsie 61

Bay City Rollers 162

BBC 119, 177, 181, 248

BBC Cumbria 52, 72

BBC Scotland 220

beta blockers 36

Bewes, Rodney 167

binge drinking 81, 83, 85, 86, 87–8

Bird, Derrick 105–8

Blease, Stephen 158, 221

Bluebird K7 185–6

Borders on Sunday 25–6, 29

Bosnian War 43, 45

Bragg, Melvyn 169–70

Brennan, Lee 170

Brexit 202–3, 244

Bristow, Eric 66

British Naturism 207, 208

Burgess, Robin 120, 147, 153, 160, 175, 197, 240

Cairncross Review 197–8

Cameron, David 167

Campbell, Donald 185, 186

Carlisle, Belinda 162–3

Carlisle City Council 175

Carlisle Living 224

Carlisle United 1, 25–32, 76, 160, 205

celebrity gossip sites 200

celebrity interviews 75, 161–74, 185

Charles, Prince of Wales 173

Chuckle Brothers 168

'churnalism' 248

CN Group 3, 4–5, 26, 58, 72, 89, 91, 178, 197, 224

  cost-cutting strategies 121, 147, 153, 160

  online journalism 117–28

  ownership 120, 147, 152–3

  see also Cumberland News; News & Star; 24: The North's National

Coates, David 157, 223

Coleman, Phil 129, 132, 225, 240

Colman, Jon 132, 251

colour pieces 40, 60, 63–70, 207–9

Comedy Carpet, Blackpool 168, 169

community contributors 157, 218–20, 247

copytakers 26

court reporting 11, 12, 26, 39, 198, 245

COVID-19 pandemic 244–5, 246–8

crime reporting 14, 18

Cumberland News xi, xii, 3–4, 18, 153

  circulation 13, 71, 117, 122, 244

Cumberland Wrestling 65–6, 92

Cumbria Life 224

Cummings, Dominic 247

Daily Mail 23, 244, 248

Daily Mirror 89, 118, 247

Daily Record 72
Daily Telegraph 85, 247
Day, Philip 105, 106
death knock 14
decline of local newspapers xii,
    179–80, 197, 198, 244
  see also redundancies; slump in
    newspaper sales
department heads daily conferences
    73, 87
digital news *see* online journalism
Dixon, Billy 61
DMG Media 248
Doctor, Ken 160
Dodd, Ken 168–9
Dowler, Milly 129
drag artists 84

Edinburgh Evening News 71, 72–8,
    193, 244
Elizabeth II, Queen 173
Elliott, Francis 191–2
European Parliament 45–6
Evening Standard 248
Evening Times 220

Facebook 118, 119, 122–8, 182, 183,
    198, 202, 227, 243, 244, 245
fake news ix, xii, 69, 125, 150, 246
feature writing 11, 17, 19, 39–48,
    121, 159, 199, 207–8
  colour pieces 40, 60, 63–70, 207–9
  profiles 40, 46–7, 49–62
Feller, Grant 198
Fenton, Amy 201, 245
Ferguson, Anthony 91, 213, 251
Firth, Colin 171
Fish (singer-songwriter) 161
Fisher, Gregor 171
floods 108–14
Floyd, George 246
football
  Carlisle United 1, 25–32, 76, 160,
    205

charity matches 96
hooligans 84
Uppies and Downies 64–5
Forth road and rail bridges 74
furloughed staff 245

Gannett 152, 177, 197–8, 234
Glass, Jimmy 76–7, 79, 80
global financial crisis (2008) 119, 121
Golden Jubilee 173
Google 118, 182, 183, 218, 237, 244
Granville, Toby 218, 238, 243
grassroots journalism 139–43
  see also community contributors
Green, Mark 158, 220–1, 233, 234,
    241
Grenfell Tower fire 198
Guardian 150, 226, 227, 235, 245,
    247, 248

Helliwell, Dave 139, 140, 149, 240
Herald 72, 220, 235
Higgins, James 150, 153
Hodges, Chas 167–8
Hodgkinson, Neil 89, 139
Hogg, Miller 147, 150–1, 152
Hold the Front Page website 157, 158,
    177, 182, 184, 197, 201, 202,
    235, 236, 252
homelessness 58–9
hospital accident and emergency units
    67
Human League 161
Hurt, John 165–7
hyperlocals 160

interviews
  celebrity 75, 161–74, 185
  profile pieces 40, 46–7, 49–62
  vox pops x, 7–8, 96–103, 163
ITV Border 4, 52, 72, 80

Japanese prisoners-of-war 75–6
Johnson, Boris 85, 86

JPI Media 181, 248

Kilroy 35, 37
Kilroy-Silk, Robert 37
King's Own Royal Border Regiment 43, 44
Kingston, Stephen 182
Knighton, Michael 25, 29–32, 160
Krankies 168

Las Vegas, Stevie 49
leader columns 144–5, 245
Lee, Stewart 161
The Likely Lads 167
Little, Tommy 186–9
local democracy reporters (LDRs) 181, 182
Longcake, Phil 226–7
Loyd, Anthony 43

McCann, Madeleine 115–16
McKeown, Les 162
McLellan, John 72, 77, 193
male strippers 84–5
Manchester United 25, 29
Marillion 161
Martin, Donald 220
Martindale, Cedric 186
May, Theresa 151, 191
Metro 149, 248
Miss World pageant 34–5
Morley, Eric 34–5
Mothers' Union 47–8
Moyles, Chris 23

naked swimming sessions 206, 208–9, 212–13
National 220
National Council for the Training of Journalists (NCTJ) 2, 11
National Union of Journalists (NUJ) 154, 175, 176, 178, 181, 197, 237, 247
New Media Investment Group 234

News & Star 3, 5, 9, 18, 153
circulation 13, 71, 117, 122, 148, 244
'Not the News and Star' Twitter account 151–2, 204, 223
News Media Association 182–3
News of the World 129
Newsquest 152–3, 154, 157, 158–9, 160, 175–9, 181, 182, 183, 184, 195, 197–8, 218, 220, 223, 224, 235–7, 243, 245, 247, 248
9/11 terrorist attacks 77, 115
North West Media Awards 131, 136, 137, 184, 233, 252
Northern Echo 157

Oakey, Phil 161
obituaries 220
O'Brien, Tim 43
Ofcom 246
online journalism 117–28, 157, 159, 182–4, 199–201, 205, 234, 238–9
clickbait ix, 158, 200, 201, 239, 248
and collapse in newspaper sales 118, 121, 122
readers' offensive and abusive comments 122–6, 127–8, 201–3, 243, 245, 246–7
web hits 158, 199, 217
web paywalls 248
Operation Market Garden 187, 188
Orton, Beth 164

Pallett, Roxanne 170–1
The Papers (BBC documentary) 220
Pellow, Marti 164–5
Penrith–Keswick rail line 186
Perry, Keith 201
phone calls 229–30
irate callers 20–1
phone hacking xi, 129
photographers 8–9, 51–2, 65, 68–9, 153, 157, 208, 220, 245, 248
PR jobs 179–80, 222

Press Association news agency 149, 233, 249
Press Gazette 177, 182, 223, 252
press officers 42
press releases 179, 183, 207–8, 248, 249
Price, Katie (Jordan) 81–3, 134
profile pieces 40, 46–7, 49–62

Raymond, Billie 84
Reach (news publisher) 118, 181, 247–8
Reed, Michael 234
Regional Press Awards 134, 135, 247
Rewcastle, Darren 105, 106–7
Richard, Cliff 35
royal family 33–4, 172–3

Saatchi & Saatchi 231
Scotsman 71, 72
Scottish Sun 247
Second World War 76, 187, 188, 189
shorthand 39
Simpson, Joe 56
Sims, Vanessa 198, 221, 223, 233, 234, 236
Skelton, Helen 170
slump in newspaper sales 118, 121, 122, 147, 148, 244
  see also decline of local newspapers
Smith, Bill 185–6
speed awareness courses 46–7
sports reporting 25–32
Spurlock, Morgan 87–8
Staines News 252
Stewart, Rod 165, 185
Stewart, Rory 202, 204
Storm Desmond 109–10, 113, 114, 160
Story, Chris 153, 154, 198–9, 217, 218, 220–1, 225, 236, 237, 238, 239
strikes 177–8
sub-editors 9, 15, 91–3, 141, 145–6, 156, 204, 239

Sun 244
Sunday News & Star 25–6, 29
Sunday Times 247
Super Size Me documentary 87–8
Sutton, Keith 5, 25, 29, 32, 35, 39, 72, 85, 86, 87, 88, 89, 144

Thomas, Ryan 170
The Times 191, 192, 245
Today 2, 3, 5, 244
Touching the Void (Joe Simpson) 56, 57
Toyah 161–2
traffic wardens 74, 126
trainee journalists 176, 181, 182, 218, 239
travel writing 95
trawler fishermen 68–9
trips abroad 43–6
Trump, Donald 191–2, 246
Trusted News Day 123
Tucci, Stanley 171
24: The North's National 148–9

Uppies and Downies 64–5

vox pops x, 7–8, 96–103, 163

Waite, Terry 173–4
Walker, Henry Faure 152–3, 178, 183, 236–7
Wessex, Sophie, Countess of 173
Weston, Simon 174
Wet Wet Wet 164
Wigton Baths 207, 208–9, 211–12
wild swimming 66–7
Wilson, Paul 107, 108

The X Factor 172

Yates, Simon 56–7
Yorkshire Evening Post 89
Young, Gordon 168

Zakir, Waseem 248